Superior Economic Performance & Profitability

Every CEO's Guide

by

VLAD TSEYTKIN
https://vladtseytkin.com

INTRODUCTION

T The role of a CEO is unique. The world of a CEO is quite different from that of the rest of humanity. A CEO may be busy with a company, but it is the responsibility of the CEO to advance the frontiers of business and take the world at large to new horizons, creating a more prosperous and wealthy society.

I've divided the material into eleven chapters. The first chapter clarifies basic assumptions of economics that are relevant to the subject. The presented picture may be simple, even simplistic, yet it's essential, as it builds a foundation. It answers the question "Why?" on a very basic level, and removes the shadow of guilt which is often subtly projected on the business world.

Practically speaking, the goal of the first chapter is to present the ultimate goal of a company, as well as the responsibility and the challenge of the CEO to take the company in that direction.

The second chapter is dedicated to building the framework and the tools. The key concept is strategy. It empowers a CEO to take the company to its ultimate goal. This is a strategy on a large scale, which we call a competitive strategy. It is both a roadmap and a tool.

While the first two chapters answer the questions "why" and "what", the remaining chapters are concerned with "how".

The third chapter focuses more on day-to-day activities and a strategy in a more localized sense of the word. The goal of a strategy on this level is meeting intermediate objectives and overcoming obstacles on the way.

The fourth chapter is putting it all together, first by revealing a unifying idea in a competitive strategy, and then by summarizing and structuring the whole framework.

The fifth chapter presents a few "light" examples and gives plenty of food for thought.

The sixth chapter connects a strategy with the bottom line - the results.

The seventh chapter defines leadership and clarifies various aspects of the position of a CEO.

The eighth chapter is dedicated to an illustration of the core idea presented in the seventh chapter. It shows one of the ways undiluted leadership can transform your business and effortlessly take it to a new level entirely.

The ninth chapter explores sales and marketing comprehensively, from the CEO's point of view.

The tenth chapter presents the science and the art of Finance to the extent that a CEO should ideally master.

The eleventh chapter introduces an advanced concept of value, as relevant to a 21st-century business. This is arguably the most important chapter in the book, and is kept until the end to linger in your mind after you finish reading.

The essence of all eleven chapters is expressed in the titles:

Chapter 1: **Why?**
Chapter 2: **What?**
Chapter 3: **Day-to-day**
Chapter 4: **From a bird's-eye view**
Chapter 5: **Examples & food for thought**
Chapter 6: **From a strategy to results**
Chapter 7: **The position of a CEO**
Chapter 8: **Leadership Labs**
Chapter 9: **The sales and marketing executive's toolbox**
Chapter 10: **Finances for a CEO**
Chapter 11: **Value revolution**
Appendix: **The CEO's Guide to The World of Ideas**

Table of
CONTENTS

CHAPTER 1

Why?

Value

W hat's the most fundamental idea in the world of business?

If you could go back in time to when the world was just created, and you were given an opportunity to introduce a revolutionary concept of business, where would you begin?

You would probably begin with the idea of VALUE.

No human being can possibly have everything he or she needs and wants.

So where exactly can we find what we need and want, but don't have now?

Well, sometimes other people have the resources we need.

However, for the most part, the needed value doesn't exist. It must be created by someone. We are all capable of creating and contributing value. Only by sharing value with each other are we allowed to succeed and prosper. Value comes in the form of products and services.

The next concept to understand is MONEY.

Let's think of money in its simplest, yet most profound and general sense: a universal medium of exchange. Money is a common denominator that enables us to quantify, compare, and exchange values, that is to say, goods and services. If not for money, we would be stuck in a world of barter, exchanging products and services directly. It would be a very different world…

Ultimate justice or ultimate injustice?

No value exists in the world in a way it could be readily and immediately consumed.

Water?

It must be packaged, transported, stored, and finally, delivered for consumption. Not to mention its requirements for preservation, purification, and quality control.

Before value can be exchanged and consumed, it must be created. Creation of value implies natural resources combined with labor, while going through specific processes to arrive at the final stage.

We're now coming closer to a simple idea. But don't be misled by its simplicity. This idea has reshaped the world many times over, inspired tens of millions, killed hundreds of millions. We need to treat the idea seriously. The quality and the quantity of your life, and the lives of those you love, depend on it.

Let's introduce and explore this idea in depth.

To create any value, we must consume the value first. After all, somebody must work, and the worker must be compensated. A worker's labor is consumed in the process of creating value. So too are the needed natural resources. This is an example of the intermediate value that is consumed for the "final" value to be created. This consumed intermediate value is invested in the creation of the final value.

When value is created economically, the resulting value, if measured, is MORE than the value invested in the creation. This is because the ADDITIONAL VALUE is created in the process. The nature of this additional value, and the idea behind it, is that very culprit, that very "simple" idea that has inspired so many, as well as claimed so many lives.

Here is a definition of the additional value, i.e. the value added in the process of value creation: "the value surplus is the excess of value produced by the labor of workers over the wages they are paid."

This is the definition given by one of the spiritual fathers of the most devastating social experiment ever tried on the face of the earth.

He considered human labor, or, more specifically, the labor of the workers, to be the source of economic value. The capitalist steals the additional value from the workers by paying the workers LESS than the value their labor has added to the goods. The capitalist steals this value surplus from the workers who actually created the surplus value to begin with.

According to this view, to restore justice, the value surplus should be taken away from the capitalist, and given back to those who created it, the workers. The disagreeing capitalist must be crushed and purged from society. The entire value surplus is going back to its source.

This "solution" surely restores ultimate justice and creates the dream life for all of us, doesn't it?

It does NOT. On the contrary.

We've hopefully learned a few history lessons, and at this point in time, we know without a shadow of a doubt that such a "noble" approach triggers untold suffering, murder, hunger, poverty, corruption on a grand scale, for hundreds of millions of innocent people.

While the history lessons are obvious, the matter is still far from obvious for many. This is because the matter is not understood on a fundamental level. This is because in theory, the "solution" still looks fair: the workers generate value surplus, and it's stolen away from them, isn't it?

Profit and loss.

Let me disrespectfully disagree with the "spiritual fathers" of the most disastrous social experiment.

"The fathers" had only one problem: they didn't bother to attempt to create the value for others. If they did, the correct answer would become obvious to them. Perhaps they were noble in their intentions, as their consciences were bothered by the poorly paid workers and by the level of poverty in their society. Yet, they were guilty of not testing their theories in real life on a small scale and analyzing the inevitable failure.

Let's stay away from history and politics.

Let's focus on the most fundamental idea that they got wrong. We're going to get it right.

What is the nature of the value surplus, of that very additional value, commonly known as "profit"?

Regardless of practical consequences, in the ideal world, in the world of truth, does it really belong to the capitalist or to the worker?

Well, it belongs to whoever creates it.

Here is the moment of truth. It's created by the capitalist. It's not created by the worker.

This is the most important and fundamental point, so let's understand it more deeply.

Before a service or a product is created, when it still exists in its potentiality, there is uncertainty involved. In fact, there are many uncertainties.

We've seen all kinds of statistics on failing businesses. According to all of them, most businesses FAIL. In fact, the vast majority fail. For example, according to Bloomberg, 8 out of 10 entrepreneurs who start businesses fail within the first 18 months.

Companies rise and fall. Industries rise and fall.

But it's not only a matter of businesses failing or succeeding. Even the most successful businesses fail in many, if not most of their projects and undertakings. It's normal. It's a part of life.

What does it mean?

It means that it's not easy to create value!

In fact, it's very difficult to create, communicate, and deliver the value that's needed and wanted by people. You work hard. You may think you are creating value, but often the customers are not coming, the created value is not in demand and is not consumed by those who should presumably need it and want it. Surprise: you've built it, but they ain't coming. If this is the case, there is no real value there - it's a loss!

Workers are employed by an entrepreneur. Workers invest their work and are compensated as agreed. Workers don't face uncertainty. Workers are very certain about their compensation. They get paid a fair value, the value they agreed on, which is a fair exchange for their contribution.

It's entrepreneurs who are facing uncertainty, and their main contribution to the value creation is its final CERTAINTY, as in the end, the value is there, certain, tangible, needed and wanted, and ready to be consumed. Moreover, regardless of the final value to be in demand, the full compensation of the workers is *certain*, as well as repayments of other debts, if any.

This certainty is a very precious commodity. An entrepreneur transforms uncertainty into certainty, by creating certain, tangible value. An entrepreneur takes uncertainty, and delivers certain value to the customers, on the way delivering certain compensation to the workers.

It's easy to see the tangible, labor-intensive contribution of the workers, which is sheltered from risks and complications, and it's so tempting to overlook the intangible, "invisible" contribution of an entrepreneur: risks and complications, uncertainties, subtle and difficult decisions in dealing with human capital, financial capital, and physical capital.

If the "spiritual fathers" attempted to create the value, i.e. actual products and services that benefited real people, they would quickly realize that the value surplus wasn't automatically created by the workers.

On the contrary, they would quickly notice in their experiments that once the capitalist is removed, the value creation becomes less and less economic, i.e. the value surplus itself is minimized, and eventually evaporates altogether. It now takes more value to produce less value, which causes the society to consume its own resources irreversibly, so that the scarcity is increased, the goods and services become less accessible, and eventually, many of them are not accessible at all. This creates corruption. The scarce value is available only to the chosen elite, those who happen to be in control of the distribution of elusive surplus to the workers.

Why is that?

That is because value, for the most part, remains in the realm of uncertainty, potentiality. Actualizing value, making it certain and tangible contains the risks, which makes it the most difficult job in the world. This job takes the skill of a different kind; it's not comparable to the skill and labor of the workers.

The basic, obvious, and foundational concept is that the very additional value, the so-called value surplus, or, simply saying, the profit, is created by the entrepreneur, by the capitalist, and is rooted in transforming uncertainty into certainty, in taking risks, in capital allocation, in navigating the labyrinth of needs and desires of the people who need products and services, to begin with.

Without any disrespect to all the employees on the planet, of course what they do is noble and must be rewarded fairly, as they contribute their time and energy, yet we must understand that employees are sheltered from balancing the risks and returns, from facing the inevitable consequences of taking the risks, and they are not bothered by complexities and difficulties of raising capital and capital allocation, because that's the domain of an entrepreneur, and that's exactly where the source of additional value is found and the root of the profit is born.

Just like loss is not the workers' loss, so too profit is not the workers' profit. They haven't created it and they don't own it. To take it away from an entrepreneur and to give to a worker is theft. It's wrong and immoral. And it inevitably leads to disasters on so many levels.

A paradoxical example

Consider the following example.

A few people are getting together to invest their own time, effort, and money into creating certain value.

They are working hard, and eventually, the value is created. A product or service finds its customer and money is flowing in.

They pay themselves their salaries and reimburse themselves for their expenses. Their creation is economically efficient, and the value surplus is being accumulated.

There is no capitalist in the picture. The workers got together and created the value themselves. Isn't it obvious that the profit belongs to them?

Not at all. In fact, if they try to pocket the profit, they would effectively transform themselves into the capitalists, and would be declared as the enemies of the state, according to the "fathers". In the real world, everything would be taken away from them, including their reputation, their freedom, and often, their lives (if you've never lived in a society which is governed by these principles, you would hardly believe this statement, but, unfortunately, it is true).

The "beauty" and the "magic" of the theory of the "fathers" is that according to them, the value surplus belongs to the working class as a whole. It doesn't belong to any specific worker, regardless of who created the value. As noble as it sounds, any particular representative of the working class must give up all the created value, regardless of how much or how little. All the value is then taken by the government to be distributed "fairly".

Contrary to these quasi-noble intentions, the deeply immoral system steals the value surplus from those who create it, i.e. from entrepreneurs, effectively crippling the value creation, and corrupting the distribution. As a result, products and services become scarce, and more and more value is accessible exclusively to the corrupt elite.

And who belongs to the elite?

Those few "lucky" ones who manage the distribution in the name of the state.

Prosperity declines and disappears. Poverty multiplies and becomes a norm. Scarcity reigns.

Let's bring it back home. Here is the bottom line. Here is the truth:

1. The value belongs to whoever creates the value.
2. The workers are compensated fairly, as per their respective employment contracts.
3. Entrepreneurs are managing and balancing the risks, and handling capital allocation. They're rewarded fairly by the profit, whenever there is profit (which is often not the case, unbeknown to the rest of the society).

The other side of profit

The ultimate goal of any business is to economically create the value, i.e. products and services which satisfy human needs.

This is true for both, B2C and B2B, as any chain of B2B companies eventually ends with B2C. At the end of any chain, there are people - not legal entities; in the end, it's all for us, human beings, to consume.

The term "economically" implies the additional value, the very value surplus we were talking about. In other words, the profit.

Profit has two sides to it. One side is obvious to all: the owners become richer. The other side is often overlooked, yet it's crucial.

The profit means that the resources R were taken from the society and consumed in the process, while in the end, the value $V = R + A$ is generated, where A is the very additional value, the profit.

This means that the society has become richer, wealthier. Profit represents the added value!

Before the value is created, the society has R amount of value in the form of raw materials, time and energy of the workers, and other resources, while in the end, the society has $V = R + A$ value, which is the value of a product or service that is instantly ready for consumption, to immediately satisfy people's needs and wants.

In a healthy society, where entrepreneurship is cherished and encouraged, the higher profit doesn't mean squeezing the worker for the sake of higher profits. Because the worker is always free to quit and find other employment with more suitable terms.

The higher profit means a more prosperous and wealthy society. This thought deserves to be meditated upon:

- the more value I create, the more value is available to others;
- the more value I create, the more value created by others I can afford to consume.

Note, "I" means every one of us. This is how wealth and prosperity multiply, while our access to wealth and prosperity is proportional to our contribution, whether we contribute as workers or as entrepreneurs.

Okay, so high profit is beneficial to the society at large, but what about the workers who produce the value?

To finalize the question about exploitation of workers, let's acknowledge that there are indeed two ways to maximize the profit:

On the dark side of capitalism, a capitalist is abusing the workers and squeezing the most out of them, to minimize the expenses needed to produce the profit.

On the bright side of capitalism, a capitalist is generously rewarding the workers by investing in them whatever their work is worth, at the same time structuring, optimizing and leveraging the processes to multiply the resulting value and achieve the highest profit.

Squeezing on the one hand, and optimizing and multiplying on the other hand.

If all we could say about these two scenarios was that the first one is immoral, while the second one is moral, we would probably be in trouble.

However, the beauty of capitalism is that the moral scenario is economically superior to the immoral one, that is to say, in the end, the second, moral scenario brings much more profit than the first, immoral one. This practically means that regardless of the source of your motivation, you're naturally incentivized to make a moral choice. That is, those who make the right choice, who optimize and multiply, will always outperform those who make the wrong choice, who squeeze and minimize.

Please note: this subject is deep and multifaceted, and our consideration is not meant to comprehensively explain all the world's problems and history. We're rather focusing on one specific dimension, leaving many other dimensions outside of our exploration. Complex political, legal, and social factors aside, since the moral choice of a capitalist is economically superior to the immoral one, sooner or later capitalism inevitably evolves and ultimately brings wealth, prosperity, and happiness to ALL.

The ultimate goal

In an advanced society, an economic value creation becomes a value on its own. People look at a company, evaluate its value creation abilities, and assign the appropriate value to those abilities. Yes, it takes a professional skill to evaluate such a value, and, in a sense, it's subjective.

At the same time, any assigned value is subjective.

When you buy bread or milk, why do you pay the price you pay?

A baker or a farmer agrees to sell it to you for that price, while you're happily ready to buy for that price. The market magically works out the prices that work for everybody and reflect "true" values, or, more precisely, define true values.

So too the company's value. The free market determines the price. As long as those who value the value creation are ready to pay that price, and current shareholders are ready to sell for that price, this is what sets the price which represents the value and corresponds to the value creation abilities of a company.

Furthermore, when a certain value is invested, it's expected to grow.

For those who are spiritually blind, this translates into greed.

For those who see beyond the physical, this means greater impact, generating even more value, more wealth and prosperity for the society.

However, this growth deserves our close attention. It shouldn't be taken for granted.

If investment R ("R" stands for resources, which implies financial capital, human capital, and physical capital) generates the value V = R + A, why would the evaluation of such a business ever change? If R->V (R produces V) costs R in the beginning, why would anybody ever pay more? Where is growth coming from?

Aside from the possibility of disrupting innovations, there are three basic factors to consider:

Over time, with more experience and skill,

1. Costs become less.
    - This is referring to the famous experience curve concept, introduced decades ago by Bruce Henderson and The Boston Consulting Group. In a nutshell, the more experience a firm has in producing a particular product, the lower its costs.
    - With minimized costs, profits increase.
2. Risks becomes less.
    - The more you do something successfully, the more confident you are, the better you are at it, the more reliable and predictable the results are.

      ○   With minimized risks, more value is created and profits increase.

3. Constantly created additional value (profit) accumulates.

      ○   More and more value is captured. The effect is compounding. With profits accumulating, additional investment opportunities multiply. Capital allocation skills become critical. With newly created capital allocated skillfully, more and more value is created, and again profits increase in relation to the initial investment R.

These factors explain why and how the value of initial investment is supposed to naturally grow over time. The business which was initially funded with investment R, is now worth more, even without disrupting innovations that may also dramatically increase the dynamics of the investments.

Hence, the ultimate goal of managing a business is superior long-term return on investment. Let's emphasize one more time: for some less advanced people, this may mean greed. For others, more advanced and at least somewhat spiritual people, this means superior prosperity and wealth-generation for the society, and, ultimately, a better, more satisfying and more accomplished life for all.

In terms of the numbers, the following indicators are very interesting to observe over time, and are very revealing:

- Gross profit margin (gross profit divided by total revenue)
- The return on assets (net earnings divided by total assets)
- Return on shareholder equity (net earnings divided by shareholder equity)
- Net earnings per share (net earnings divided by number of shares)

The ultimate indicator is arguably net earnings per share. However, all four, and many others, give a fuller picture of how the company is doing, how value creation is enriching the world, creating a prosperous and wealthy society.

The truth is, the quantitative indicators of superior economic performance is a subject on its own. The art of finance is a wonderful and subtle area. The very same company, the very same business activities and results may be presented totally differently by two finance professionals. A CEO must be keenly aware of the business phenomena that cause these differences. Assumptions, estimates, and interpretations behind the income statement, the balance sheet, and the cash flow statement, their meaning and implications should be fully understood. (The subject of finances is covered more fully in Chapter 10.)

Now, as we've realized that the ultimate goal of managing a company is a superior long-term return on investment, we're entering a new area: who is in charge of achieving this goal, and how can this be done?

In just two words,

Who?

    CEO - A Chief Executive Officer.

How?

Strategy - More specifically, a competitive strategy (this term was introduced by Michael Porter; there is a whole world behind this term that needs to be recognized and explained, which we will do right after introducing the very important frameworks first).

CHAPTER 2

What?

Competitive advantage

The most important concept for ANY company in general, and for a CEO in particular, is "competitive strategy". It's a competitive strategy that gives a company competitive advantage.

However, the term "competitive strategy" is somewhat misleading. I wish another term would be coined for that.

Why?

Because it really is the backbone, the core, the definition of the business.

Yet, paradoxically, it's not ALWAYS needed.

So, is it the backbone, or is it not always needed? Isn't it a contradiction?

To achieve clarity, let's understand first who needs a Competitive Strategy and who doesn't.

- **Context 1.** Scarcity of resources and solutions on the one hand; and abundance of unfulfilled needs, desires, and potential customers on the other hand. In its extreme, such a context is commonly encountered in a socialist society, but in softer variations, it can be found anywhere.

- In such a context, no competitive strategy is needed. Practically speaking, a customer is chasing after a value provider, so the only job of a value provider is to generate and deliver the value. Paradoxically, it's the customer who competes for the resources and solutions. It's the customer who needs to create the strategy to find and access the value provider, sometimes even for the most basic needs.
- **Context 2.** Resources and solutions are plentiful, which, practically speaking, simply means that a COMPETITION exists in the industry. In this context, it's a value provider who is "chasing" after a customer, not the other way around.
  - Under the circumstances, a strategy is a must. It implies a unique position which involves a unique combination of activities; creating unique value in a unique way.
  - Having a good strategy means earning the right to serve your customer. In an advanced capitalist economy, serving a customer becomes a precious privilege.
  - Competition creates an amazing society where people are offered many solutions which help them satisfy their many needs and desires in so many different ways. In contrast to a socialist economy, the difficulty is shifted to the other side: it becomes difficult to offer, to serve, while the consumption becomes effortless. The main challenge of a consumer is to choose, not to find, while the main challenge of a value provider is to be found and to be chosen.

Competitive Strategy sins:

- **Sin #1.** No strategy at all.
  - Most companies don't have a strategy. Well, they may think they do, but they don't.
- **Sin #2.** An implicit strategy.

- An implicit strategy may be incomplete (implemented only partially);
- Or inconsistent, when multiple contradicting strategies may be in place at the same time. This will:
  - Confuse customers.
  - Diminish efficiencies.
  - Minimize effectiveness.
  - Cause many troubles on different levels, resulting in low profitability, if any.
- **Sin #3**. Strategy is equal to operational effectiveness.
  - This is mixing up strategic and tactical approaches.
  - Doing right things is strategic VS. Doing things right is tactical
    - Being different means performing different activities, or similar activities in different ways (this is strategic) VS. Performing similar activities better (this is tactical).
      - While strategic approach gives you long-term competitive advantage, a tactical approach doesn't. Tactical advantage is short-lived and can be (and usually is) easily copied by competitors.
- **Sin #4**. Company's strategy equals marketing strategy. Or even worse, a strategy equals a marketing slogan.
- **Sin #5**. Misunderstanding the essence of a strategy: trying to be the BEST instead of trying to be DIFFERENT, UNIQUE.

The Competitive Strategy ingredients are:

1. **Value** (the benefit to people or companies; can be more value or less value - value can be maximized or minimized vertically or horizontally - the choice is yours to make.)
2. **Target** (the target audience; who the value is for; the audience can be more narrow or wider - the choice is yours to make.)

  ○ For example, little value to many customers OR a lot of value to few customers.

3. **Needs or Wants** (the exact needs or wants of the target audience the value is addressing; can address more needs or less needs; in comparison to the rivals, the needs can represent a subset or a superset; the choice is yours to make.)

4. **Access** (how exactly the target audience is accessing the value; the communication chain and the delivery and consumption mechanisms are clarified.)

Industry

A company lives in an ecosystem. It loosely correlates to its industry, and is described by the main forces that set the stage and the context for your business. **These Forces give shape to a Competitive Strategy and generally correspond to its structure:**

1. VALUE-related:
 a. **Other** value providers
  i. Existing (rivalry)
  ii. Future / potential: new entrants (practically speaking, what's involved in becoming a new player in the market.)
 b. **Alternative** value providers, i.e. alternative ways to satisfy the same needs (substitute products & services.)
 c. **Value creation** and quality control (partners, **suppliers**, processes; just what it takes to create and validate the value.)
2. CUSTOMERS-related.
3. NEEDS-related.
4. ACCESS-related.

Why do we call them forces?

That's because they can be big and powerful, or small and vulnerable; they can be easy for us to handle, or difficult; they can be cooperative or confrontational, friendly or competitive.

When they are "big and powerful" relative to our company, this means that in our relationship with them, they have an upper hand, and we will be forced to some extent to sacrifice our profitability when facing their power in negotiations or their purchasing power.

Needs-related forces are different, though you can surely notice a common denominator: people (or companies) experience their needs with different intensity. They may feel vulnerable and desperate, or may feel relatively neutral, or anywhere in-between. The closer they are to being neutral, the stronger they are; in a sense, the more power they may manifest in negotiations.

A good insight into the five forces is very important because they provide the ecosystem and the context for our business, and they shape our competitive strategy.

They are usually classified as:

1. Competitors
2. New entrants
3. Substitutes
4. Suppliers
5. Customers

But I prefer the classification that is parallel to the structure of competitive strategy, the way I presented it.

A Good Strategy:

- A good strategy results in superior economic performance. The goal of a strategy is superior profitability.
- A good strategy is not only simple; a good strategy is obvious (unfortunately, often only after the fact!)
- If a company has multiple business units or product lines, each one may or may not require a strategy on its own. The strategy

of a particular unit or a line may or may not belong to a higher-level umbrella strategy.

An existing strategy VS. creating a new strategy.

It usually takes quite an effort and a few iterations to even understand an existing strategy in an existing, already successful company, let alone creating a new winning strategy for a startup.

In terms of its benefits, a great, explicit, clearly formulated and communicated strategy is crucial for both: for a startup to achieve success, as well as for a mature company to reach a next level of profitability and increase shareholder value.

In terms of its essence, a strategy binds all the aspects and activities together, makes a business WHOLE, and is a foundation of everything that happens, or doesn't happen, in the business and around it.

When do we work on a competitive strategy?

So what place does a competitive strategy have in your business, in terms of your time and effort?

To arrive at a great strategy, it's surely healthy to debate and brainstorm ideas and possibilities. However, at a certain point, the debate must stop. Appropriate decisions are made, and the strategy is set.

The word "decision" is crucial here. Let me emphasize this. Strategy by consensus is not a good strategy. A good strategy is NOT about a compromise. It's about the choices you make as a CEO, and clarity the choices bring.

From this moment on, the discussion should be "how to do it really well."

Perhaps one day, we may be compelled to review our strategy. Is it still viable?

Hopefully, this happens very rarely. Until we decide to re-evaluate the strategy, we can't discuss it over and over again. We must be busy implementing and communicating the strategy.

The structure of a company

- **Shareholders**, owner(s) - Appoint board of directors. Primary activity: voting. Primary decision: initial capital allocation (i.e. a decision to invest in this company).

- **Board of directors** - Appoint a CEO, as well as oversee the results of the CEO's activities and giving the feedback; serve as the highest authority for a CEO. Primary activity: support and feedback loop (both, reinforcing and balancing) for a CEO.

- **CEO** - Achieving superior ROI for the shareholders. Primary activity: developing the vision and the strategy; capital allocation; managing the executives; managing the risks and developing the opportunities. Primary activity in one word: decision-making.

- **Executives** - Primary focus: objectives set by the CEO and obstacles on the way to achieving those objectives. Primary activity: deciding on the strategies to meet the objectives and overcome the obstacles; managing the workers in the process of implementing the strategies. Managing implies the following: defining the roles (the framework, rules, conditions, activities), appointing employees to the role, setting the objectives to achieve, overseeing the activities and the results, and providing the feedback.

- **Workers** - Primary focus: tasks. Primary activity: "doing work". Perform the activities within the framework under the executives' management.

Please note: all five roles are always present in all the stages. In a simplest case of a one-person startup, all five may be combined in one person, an entrepreneur, and gradually, as the company grows, the roles are split up and assigned to new people.

The company's organization naturally follows the main functions. Here are the main functions which apply to most companies:

- Overseeing & managing all
- Product development (from an idea to being ready for fulfillment)
  - Envision, Design, Develop and Create product or service
- Marketing
- Sales
- Fulfillment
- Supportive functions
  - Operations
  - Human resources
  - Managing finances & accounting
  - Customer service
  - Information Technology
  - Data management

Accordingly, here are the executives whose roles correspond to the functions:

- CEO
  - Product development manager
  - Marketing manager
  - Sales manager
  - Fulfillment manager
  - Operations manager
  - H/R manager
  - Accounting manager
  - Customer service manager
  - IT Manager
  - Data management manager

Until a certain point in the company's development, all the executives usually report to the CEO. However, as a company grows, some "secondary" functions may be brought under operations, with an operation manager (COO) taking a load from a CEO, for example:

- CEO
  - Product development manager
  - Marketing manager
  - Sales manager
  - H/R manager
  - Operations manager
    - Fulfillment manager
    - Accounting manager
    - Customer service manager
    - IT Manager
    - Data management manager

As a company grows further, more "secondary" supportive functions may be brought under operations, with a CEO primarily focusing on profit centers, for example (following Michael Masterson):

- CEO
  - Profit center manager
    - Product development manager
    - Marketing manager
    - Sales manager
  - Profit center manager
    - Product development manager
    - Marketing manager
    - Sales manager
  - ………....
  - Operations manager
    - Fulfillment manager
    - H/R manager
    - Accounting manager
    - Customer service manager

- IT Manager
- Data management manager

A profit center is a unit of a company treated almost as a separate business. The term was coined by Peter Drucker who later "took it back", but it was too late: the term has been used extensively since then. The term may be more or less appropriate, as per Peter Drucker, but the concept is very important. Profit centers introduce flexibility, ease accountability, make a company scalable, facilitate more intelligent capital allocation, take risk management to the next level, and allow executives to achieve greatness, as a profit center manager's role is one of a mini-CEO.

Company's operations support profit centers by providing common infrastructure. However, as Michael Masterson has pointed out, at times it may make sense for a profit center to outsource certain projects or functions, even if they are provided by the company's operations. Practically speaking, it would rarely be the case, but such an option is always there, which helps focus on efficiency and effectiveness, as well as putting healthy pressure on the company's operations and shaping up the company as a whole.

The four stages - the life cycle of a company

When analyzing a business, understanding the framework is essential. It shows us how to think about business, how to view it, gives us a way of systematically putting together parts and pieces and recognizing the whole.

The first framework concerns the life cycle of a business. It was introduced and brilliantly analyzed by Michael Masterson. From the moment of its birth, there are four stages a business goes through:

1. **The first stage.** Creating initial, minimal value which is actually consumed by those who it's created for.
   - The main objective is the first sale, made profitably and consistently replicated.
   - This stage generally implies $0 - $1M revenue; a few employees are directly reporting to an entrepreneur.

- We should really use the term "CEO" instead of "entrepreneur" here. Practically speaking, it's usually an entrepreneur, the one who started the business, yet an entrepreneur is playing the role of a CEO, a chief executive who is actually running the business.
  - The main activity: attempting to sell. To oversimplify, just try to sell something to someone, and understand precisely what you've sold, to whom, why, and how.

2. **The second stage.** Extending and expanding an initial offer by introducing additional products and services.
   - The flow of customers is no longer a challenge: this was taken care of in the first stage. Now the challenge is to extend and expand by creating more offers - more value.
   - This stage generally implies $1M - $10M revenue; a few employees are directly reporting to those who directly report to a CEO.
   - Create products and services, market and sell, create, market and sell, bring customers back and sell.

3. **The third stage.** Organize, proceduralize, templatize, optimize, fine-tune, multiply.
   - If we had to pick one word, it would be "multiply" which means leveraging what we've created in the first two stages. Of course, to successfully leverage without being overwhelmed, we would have to organize better, create well-defined procedures and templates, optimize and fine-tune, etc.
   - This stage generally implies $10M - $50M revenue; the third wave of employees is hired: those who report to those who report to those who report directly to a CEO.
   - Efficiency, automation, exceptional human resources are some of the key areas to focus on.

4. **The fourth stage.** This stage generally implies $50M+ revenue, and the executives, particularly the CEO, are distinctly independent from the owners (shareholders).

   ○ Continue running operations efficiently, yet the main focus becomes deploying cash generated by operations. Superior capital allocation skills is the key. It's tempting for a CEO to delegate this function to somebody else, like a CFO. However, this is where a CEO really shines and has a chance to create an extraordinary, superior organization. The subject has been investigated in-depth, with great examples, by William Thorndike.

   ○ A CEO has to become fluent and really master the following five things, as five functions of capital allocation:
      ▪ Investing in existing operations
      ▪ Acquiring other businesses
      ▪ Issuing dividends
      ▪ Paying debt
      ▪ Repurchasing stock

Understanding which of the four stages your company is going through gives you clarity and advantage. Each stage is unique, having its own flavor and unique set of strategies.

Strategy dynamics throughout the company life cycle

A strategy is always a strategy, regardless of the size of the company or its stage. However, there is a very important distinction which needs to be clarified.

What's the most essential difference between the four stages of the company life cycle?

The revenue and the number of employees are good indicators, but they are rather coincidental. They are not definitive.

The main difference is the level of uncertainty.

In the beginning, all you have is assumptions. You don't know anything with certainty. Even though you may have an idea, and perhaps even the product or service, you still don't know what in the end you are going to sell, to whom, how, and why exactly they're going to buy.

That's why in the first stage, you sell, sell, and sell, or, more precisely, you try, try, and try until you sell. The ultimate goal of the first stage is to sell something to somebody, and then to try to understand how it happened and why, and replicate it. What comes out in the end may correlate to your original plan more or less - often less than more.

Your initial strategy is almost guaranteed not to survive.

There are two types of a strategy: pre-strategy, and post-strategy. Pre-strategy is an assumptive strategy; it's based on assumptions. The uncertainty level is high.

You go ahead, try, test, fine-tune, and again, try, test, and fine-tune, until the results are better than before. Now, looking back, after the fact, you re-formulate the strategy. It's no longer based on assumptions. It's based on facts, or, more precisely, on your interpretation of the facts. It may be drastically different, or at least somewhat different from your initial, assumptive strategy. At this point, if your attempt has been successful, you don't really create the strategy, but rather extract, discover the strategy that worked.

This is what post-strategy is about. Post-strategy is a strategy derived from looking back and understanding what happened, how, and why. You still make assumptions, but not as many as before. A new challenge is now to interpret the facts correctly. This may become quite subtle, as there are usually many interpretations available. It may take a few iterations until you're satisfied with the results, yet the level of uncertainty is lower on each next step.

Does it mean that a pre-strategy is unnecessary, and the best approach is to try to sell something to somebody without a well-defined strategy?

No! This would be wrong.

You ALWAYS need to have a well-defined, clear strategy before an action. At the same time, you must be aware of the level of uncertainty, what's based on facts and what's based on assumptions. Is anything based on facts at all? Are you using all the facts at your disposal?

You must always be ready to fine-tune, upgrade, or even drastically change the strategy when necessary, based on the feedback loop.

Every phase begins with a pre-strategy, and ends with a post-strategy. You need a strategy in the beginning, as well as you need to re-evaluate it at the end.

Relative to each other, a pre-strategy is an assumptive strategy, while a post-strategy is an after-the-fact strategy.

To oversimplify, in terms of the four stages of the business life cycle, 75% of the eventually successful strategy is developed in stage 1, and the remaining 25% is completed in stage 2.

When entering stage 3, for the most part, the difference between pre- and post-strategy is no longer applicable. By this time, the strategy has been formulated and "canonized". In this sense, the 1st stage is very entrepreneurial, the 2nd stage is more or less entrepreneurial, and the 3rd stage is anti-entrepreneurial. In the 3rd stage, relative to the strategy, there is no place for innovation, but only for tactical and quantitative improvements.

The strategy has become solid and now serves as a foundation for building an extraordinary company. At this point, a solid, inflexible strategy makes the company strong.

However, there is a danger here. The source of strength is becoming the root of weakness which may eventually bring about the company's demise. Let's zoom in here, as this is crucial to understand.

Over time, a company evolves from high-risk, high-uncertainty, to low risk, low uncertainty. However, at any given moment, it's not a matter of choice. It's a matter of being perceptive, becoming aware of the risk level that is most beneficial at the moment.

Each of the following two mistakes may have devastating consequences for the company:

1. Making decisions out of certainty in the place of uncertainty;
2. Choosing to imagine uncertainty in the midst of certain environs.

Over the life cycle of a company, there are four types of high-risk, high-uncertainty situations:

1. In the very beginning, in the 1st stage.
   - Uncertainty is extreme. Risks are high. Trial-and-error period is inevitable. No matter how sure you are about being successful, the chances of success are slim. You eventually succeed only if you don't give up, after going through a few iterations. This stage never goes as planned. It always takes more investment than you thought it would take, whether you invest time, effort, or money. In this stage, a prayer may work better than everything else, but only after you try everything else. Feels very vulnerable. Total lack of control over the outcome is not for the weak of heart.
   - The same equation also concerns the 2nd stage, but not as much. The risks in the 2nd stage are generally lower.
2. A disruptive idea or a technology is entering the stage (externally; it's being developed outside of your company).
   - This is especially tricky when your company is in the 3rd stage, with everything in place and working. Suddenly, you face a potential threat: an idea or a technology that may change everything. But it's too early to be sure about it. It's uncertain. You can't possibly ignore it, yet you can't blindly embrace it either. You don't know.
     - There is an inherent contradiction here.
       - Your strategy is set. It's proven and effective.

- The processes and values in your company are configured around certainty. Yet a new idea or a new technology is presenting a highly uncertain opportunity. If you try to blend the opportunity into your existing value chain, the opportunity will most probably choke and die.

- While the overall objective in the company at this stage may be the profit, when it comes to new ideas and technologies, the objective is to try, to test, to probe, and to vary.

- As the resources are generally allocated based on the bottom line, a new beginning may just starve to death for a lack of resources. The resource allocation must be handled distinctly, differently in comparison to the rest of the organization.

3. Disruptive ideas or technology are being developed (internally).
    - Everything just said about disruption coming from outside applies in this case too.
    - There isn't enough data about this new idea or technology. It's not driven by market demand. It's not clear if there is a market for it altogether. It may be tried in different markets, as it may be relevant to tiny insignificant markets first.
    - Everything is fluid about this new opportunity.
    - When such an opportunity is managed in the context of the rest of the organization, based on the principles of lower risks and lower uncertainty, even the very best managerial techniques will lead to failure.
    - In the context of disruptive technologies, this subject has been explored by Clayton Christensen in great detail.

4. In the mature, 4th stage of business development.

   o In this happy stage (as it's a big deal for a company to get to this stage), capital allocation is the key. In the words of Michael Masterson, "you have to become entrepreneurial again". This means that you must consider various opportunities, and some of these opportunities will inevitably be high-risk, high-uncertainty. How will you handle them?

   o There is an array of decisions to be made about every opportunity that comes your way. You can't afford to ignore them!

   - You can try to develop them internally.
     - For the reasons already outlined, ideally, there should be a separate unit, a separate team assigned to the task.
   - You can start another organization, a spinoff, around the opportunity.
   - You can acquire another organization which has already advanced the opportunity.
     - How will you manage an acquired organization? It's tempting to integrate management to cut costs, yet such integration would eliminate the essential difference in the levels of uncertainty, which is a setup for failure.

Regardless of the form and the structure, there be a common denominator. The following should always be kept in mind:

Every opportunity, every unit of the business always has its own risk and uncertainty level, from low to high, and anywhere in between. Different levels must be taken into consideration a) by developing a strategy on its own for some opportunities, even if within the boundaries of an overall strategy in place; b) by having a special resource allocation procedure to avoid competition for resources, as there should be no direct competition between certainty and uncertainty; c) by realizing that there is an intrinsic inconsistency, even a contradiction to the mainstream processes and values of the company, and being comfortable about it.

On a more fundamental level, the full spectrum of risk-taking, from low to high, has its place in an organization. However, any given risk and uncertainty level requires a special, corresponding mindset - in management, and in execution. Levels don't mix well. Care should be taken to keep them apart in a harmonious manner.

CHAPTER 3

Day-to-day

A Strategy (vs. A Competitive Strategy).

Now, as we've explained the meaning of the term "competitive strategy", we have to distinguish a competitive strategy from a more basic, "regular" use of the term strategy. Just to emphasize the difference, just for a minute, let's call a common, more narrow meaning of the term "strategy" a collaborative strategy.

What is a **Collaborative Strategy** in contrast to a more global and definitive **Competitive Strategy?**

- A Competitive Strategy defines a company (or a unit, or a line of business) and enables a company to thrive in a solution-rich economy. In a sense, it's the way to "earn" a customer in an environment where customers are relatively scarce, due to fierce competition, which is the side effect of a solution-rich society.
- A collaborative strategy is more localized and time- and context-dependent. It comes to life when we're having difficulties, or facing obstacles in meeting a certain objective.
- A collaborative strategy, or simply a strategy, means a coherent approach, which enables us to overcome a specific challenge, or to meet a specific objective.

So, when do we need a collaborative **strategy?**

- We need it whenever we have challenges to overcome, or objectives to meet.
- We need it whenever we identify the biggest **challenge,** or the most important goal or **objective.**

What is a good collaborative **strategy?**

1. Understanding the nature of the challenge or the nature of the obstacle which prevents us from meeting the objective.
2. Creating a Guiding Policy that will guide us towards the desired results.
3. Designing a set of coherent actions or activities to overcome the challenge or meet the objective.
4. Understanding the main distinctions and the aspects of the business, such as:
   a. Creating value (which includes precise matching of the value to the corresponding wants and needs).
   b. Marketing (creating prospects, which implies catching attention and developing interest).
   c. Selling (converting prospects into customers who will consume the value).
   d. Delivering value (satisfying customers' needs or wants; helping them achieve their goals).
   e. Handling finances (capital allocation etc.).

Creating value, marketing, selling, delivering value, and handling finances are 5 interconnected components of any business. The division of a business into these 5 components has profound implications.

Any problem, challenge, obstacle, or an objective will always belong to one of the 5 mentioned areas of a business. It's of extreme importance to understand which one it is, in every case. This helps us achieve clarity and select or design an appropriate strategy.

It's very helpful to be aware of further distinctions to formulate the strategy requirements. For example, when it comes to marketing and sales, the following distinctions are crucial:

1. You want MORE customers.
2. You want BETTER quality customers.
3. You want your customers to spend EXTRA money with you.
4. You want your customers to COME BACK again and again, and to REFER others.
5. You want to LEVERAGE your activities to multiply the results.

This is my version of Jay Abraham's groundbreaking and brilliant "Three ways to grow a business" concept (focusing on the three distinct areas: more clients; increasing the size of the transaction; increasing the frequency of each client's purchase).

This practically means that you would never look for a strategy to just grow revenue or increase your customer base in general. You would have to be more specific than that. Namely, you would look for a strategy to meet one of the five mentioned objectives. This is because each aspect of revenue generation has its own set of proven strategies, and it's so much more rewarding to explicitly target one aspect at a time.

There are many ways to break an organization's activities into strategically relevant interconnected pieces, so that you can see a fuller picture and make corrections appropriately. This is a useful strategic approach which is generally called <u>a value chain</u>.

Theoretically speaking, **a value chain is a systemic view of a business**.

Practically speaking, a business is simply a set of activities, and **a value chain is nothing more than a series of distinctions which create a meaningful model of your business and help you classify the activities BASED on their relationship to the VALUE your company creates, communicates, and delivers**. A well-understood and carefully designed value chain allows you to effectively laser-focus on various aspects of the business in the most meaningful and practically useful manner.

CHAPTER 4

A bird's-eye view

Look for one where you have many

The competitive advantage framework is very simple, and this very simplicity may tempt us to overlook two things: the brilliance of its creator, Michael Porter, and its profound implications for our business, if we implement it thoughtfully, with full attention to detail.

Its four ingredients: value, target, needs, and access, need to be considered carefully, and their scope, extent, and borderlines should be designed masterfully. In fine-tuning these four ingredients lies a secret of uniqueness, a recipe of infinite possibilities to differ from your competitors, which means infinite possibilities to satisfy your customers' needs and wants in a unique way.

However, for the maximum effectiveness, before you consider the four ingredients, you have to conceive one idea, one concept which is unique to you, which will rather manifest itself in the four ingredients later on. This is something Michael Porter didn't focus on. Why didn't he?

Because the idea of the ONE idea was obvious to him; his job and his contribution was to show the structure of the ONE idea, so he did just that by splitting it up into components.

But for us, it would be a mistake to focus on MANY while overlooking ONE unifying idea, the one that ties everything else together.

Practically speaking, if the ONE idea is not apparent, it may be easier for you to first consider multiple variations by looking at the four components of a competitive strategy, and only then come up with one unique idea, but in any case, as a rule, wherever you have many components, there must be one all-encompassing idea. Always look for one where you have many.

Richard Rumelt demonstrated this beautifully, and brought a few great examples.

Consider Southwest Airlines.

There are many unique activities that could be found in what the company was doing from its inception, on the way to becoming wildly successful and profitable. However, in looking at MANY things, it's very difficult to discern ONE unique thing, its definitive idea.

Low cost, fast turnaround time by the gate, one airplane model only (Boeing 737), short-distance flights only, very basic amenities only, nothing fancy, no assigned seats, no baggage transfers, no meals, brutally inhospitable, low fare, frequent departures, non-busy airports only (avoiding crowded airports, i.e. those that give the most business to the airlines), and many more. All these features were open and known to all. Some features made some sense, other features made no sense at all, but in any case, it's almost impossible to recognize ONE thing, the ONE brilliant idea that all of the features express.

Let's find it.

The offer was introduced in three cities in Texas: Dallas, Houston, and San Antonio.

How do you travel between these cities?

Well, you travel by car. It's a 4-hour drive. There were flights between these cities before Southwest, but due to many factors, it was relatively uncommon to travel by air. Airplane wasn't something you would think of first when you thought of travelling from Dallas to Houston.

Southwest went ahead and changed that: by attacking those factors, Southwest introduced a 40-minute flight to replace a 4-hour drive. Southwest didn't care about other airlines, and didn't even compete with them. The company aligned itself and competed with ground transportation instead. Other airlines were irrelevant to Southwest!

If you look again at all those features that Southwest introduced, you can clearly see how they all express one simple idea - a preferred travel by air instead of ground transportation, a convenient, pleasant, and efficient 40-minute flight to replace a 4-hour drive.

Once the idea is born and crystallized, you can formulate the four ingredients of the competitive strategy much easier, as you already know what you're looking for.

Also, you can go through your whole value chain, adjusting all the business activities to comply with the main idea, as well as with the four competitive strategy ingredients. No feature, no factor, no change is random. Everything fits into a larger picture; everything is a part of a master plan.

And this is something your competitors don't see. Yes, it's open and obvious to all, yet they don't see it because it's an idea, and it's an idea which is very difficult to create or extract from a pile of seemingly unconnected activities. Truthfully, I am not even sure what's more difficult: to create such an idea for a new business, or to discern the idea behind an established successful business.

Your competitors may see random features and activities in place, yet nothing makes much sense to them; they are at a loss; and any attempt to copy your value chain is inherently unsuccessful, because they are missing the WHOLE, while trying to duplicate parts.

That's why some airlines failed miserably when they tried to copy Southwest. Moreover, they didn't understand why they were failing; after all they duplicated the activities which were open and obvious to all!

Yet, even though the pieces were there, the whole wasn't there. Their failure was inevitable.

And even if they do understand your idea, if for example you would tell them the idea clearly and explain it fully, they would still be at a loss, as their business is not based on this idea. The more established and successful they are, the less sense it makes for them to readjust all their policies and operations to a new idea and discard everything they were based on until then.

Similarly, as per Peter Drucker, Cadillac never competed with other car manufacturers. Cadillac wasn't about transportation, despite being a car. Cadillac competed with diamond dealers!

When you consider ANY very successful company, besides a great competitive strategy, they ALWAYS have a great definitive idea which the strategy is based on, the idea which is the root to everything else.

The problem is, it's very difficult to discern what the idea is exactly.

Moreover, a company may be very successful due to a combination of a variety of factors, yet they themselves don't necessarily clearly understand the idea behind their own success! The world of ideas is the most impactful, the most rewarding for value creation, yet the conceptual universe is very difficult to navigate, let alone skillfully correlate it with the physical world.

Whether you observe a startup, or an established company, you see many features, activities, practices, and policies in place, yet the many remains many. To understand what the idea is takes tremendous effort. It's like trying to recreate a crime based on a few clues left on a crime scene.

There are so many clues. You deal with almost overwhelming complexity.

Yet, once the main idea is understood, you're facing an astounding simplicity.

Does your business have such a definitive idea, which organizes everything else around it, along with a competitive strategy and a value chain?

CHAPTER 5

Examples & food for thought

I t's fascinating to observe companies and attempt to perceive their competitive strategies. I would compare this to a journey. There are so many discoveries on the way.

The objective of such an exercise is not to discover ultimate truth about the companies. In fact, the objective is subjective, in the sense that it doesn't really matter if what you discover is real or not. Let me explain.

First, there is no objective reality here. We dive into the conceptual universe, and we draw analogies, generalize, and build conceptual frameworks and models.

Second, these discoveries help you expand your mind, and come up with great ideas that you can use successfully in your industry, in your business.

Third, just because you have detected a competitive strategy of a certain company, it doesn't mean that the executives of the company are explicitly aware of it. It's not entirely uncommon to have success without understanding its recipe, though of course, with a competitive strategy being explicit, the chances of success are considerably higher, and the chances of survival and continual success are much greater too.

A note of caution: when you consider your own company and there are practical consequences, you'd better be rooted in reality firmly. When I said that the reality didn't matter, I rather meant to say that it doesn't matter until a certain point. This point is when you start applying the ideas to your industry, to your business, to your situation.

The "technology" of observation and analysis is simple: observe and apply the formula:

Competitive strategy = {value, target, needs, access} + Idea.

Please note, the idea should really be the first, as it's the idea that manifests in four dimensions of a competitive strategy. However, mining for the idea is a tedious process, and it's almost never possible to extract it before all the four dimensions are carefully considered.

With that in mind, let's consider an example: UBER.

Target: service providers and their customers (in this case, for a particular service - namely, car rides). More generically, participants of a transaction.

Value: a platform which facilitates and handles a transaction. The value has various aspects to it.

Generally, a service provider (a taxi service in this case) has to do many supportive, secondary activities, in addition to actually providing a service. For example, marketing, getting leads, calculating prices, negotiating prices, converting leads into customers, calculating routes, coordinating work for multiple customers, invoicing, handling financial transactions, working out regulatory requirements and legalities.

A customer (a passenger in this case) has an extensive job too: finding a service provider, choosing, due diligence (assessing the risks of dealing with a particular service provider), watching out if the price is fair, paying, handling various issues and disputes.

The platform Uber provides handles everything. Literally everything - including all the supportive activities. All a driver has to do is click a button, and give somebody a ride. All a passenger has to do is click a button, and take a ride. They don't have to get involved in anything else; everything else is done quickly, efficiently, on autopilot.

An essential part of the platform is a deal structure. This is something that's easily overlooked. Drivers and passengers enter well-defined, perfectly-structured and balanced business relationships. Even though it's invisible, and neither party, practically speaking, has full awareness of it, the deal structure is such that it results in a superb experience for both, drivers and passengers.

This ideal deal structure is counter-intuitive, as before Uber existed, when drivers and passengers had to work out their relationships by themselves, the spontaneous deal structure often created a miserable experience. Sometimes for a driver, sometimes for a passenger, and sometimes for both. It clearly didn't work well way too often. Each party was trying to possess and exercise maximum power in the relationship, and with one party at a disadvantage, both parties suffered in many ways.

And, of course, their reputation system. Arguably pioneered by Amazon, it no longer requires an explanation. Can anybody imagine shopping without a transparent and fair rating system?

Needs: hassle-free car transportation (which means providing a ride for a driver, and finding and taking a ride for a passenger).

Access: ONE entry point - in this case, a convenient, intuitive app on a smartphone. For both, a driver and a passenger, the experience is literally a click away. Accessible anytime, anywhere, in a unified manner.

Idea: There is no correct answer to the question about the one main idea behind the strategy. There may be many correct answers. Here is one version of an idea:

It's the concept which I call "CORE ACTIVITY ONLY - anytime, anywhere, in a unified manner, through ONE entry point".

This means that when one party wants to provide a service, and the other party wants to use a service, the ONLY thing they must still do is for a service provider to give a ride, and for a customer to get into a car and allow oneself to be transported. The core activity in this case means, for a driver, giving a ride, and, for a passenger, taking a ride.

The platform handles everything else, leaving out only the core activity itself.

Not only does one not have TO DO anything else, but one doesn't even have TO WORRY or even THINK about anything else.

Hence, I've captured the idea as "CORE ACTIVITY ONLY - anytime, anywhere, in a unified manner, through ONE entry point".

Now, let's put together what we've got (without emphasizing what an actual service is):

- CORE ACTIVITY ONLY - anytime, anywhere, in a unified manner, through ONE entry point:
  - Facilitating and handling transactions between service providers and their customers.
  - Providing ALL secondary, supportive activities.
  - Deal structure.
  - Network effect (anytime & anywhere.)
  - Reputation system.

I don't know about you, but now that I see it this way, it reminds me of other companies, like Airbnb, Amazon, eBay, Alibaba, etc. - for the respective services they provide to their customers (though not a 100% match, a few elements do overlap impressively.)

For example, Airbnb:

- CORE ACTIVITY ONLY - in a unified manner, through ONE entry point:
  - Facilitating and handling transactions between service providers and their customers.
  - Providing ALL secondary, supportive activities.
  - Deal structure.
  - Reputation system.

Interestingly, even though we've considered only one specific example, the strategy we've extracted can be so useful for so many different types of business.

The truth is, I gave this example just to show one possible direction to understand the ONE idea. However, we've come up with rather superficial understanding here. See the Appendix for the analysis which uncovers the heart of the matter.

CHAPTER 6

From a strategy to results

"I don't want a strategy! I want results!"

Just the words an expert strategist wants to hear from a CEO!

These situations leave a place for humor, but at the same time the conceptual confrontation between a strategy and results is deeper than it seems to be on the surface.

Decades ago, during my university years, I got involved with Artificial Intelligence. AI wasn't even nearly close to what it is today, but even then, it had its fascinations.

I was particularly impressed by a few-hours-long presentation dedicated to a strategy of the mind of a hungry person who woke up in the middle of a night and decided to go for a snack. The journey to a fridge, including the scene of staring at the fridge's content and trying to choose, involved a complex strategy which took a few hours to discuss, and even then, it wasn't understood clearly.

What's the lesson?

The lesson is not to convince you to start designing the strategy for your next snack time.

The lesson is that EVERYTHING has a strategy to it. Without exceptions. The only question is if it's worth to make a strategy explicit, or to leave it implicit, hidden in the depth of the mind.

If a strategy is an arbitrary course of action, vaguely based on a combination of somewhat-related experience and intuition, then it's difficult to see any benefits of an explicit strategy. What comes from vagueness and intuition should probably remain as such.

However, to answer this question with confidence, let's understand how a strategy emerges. It's simple, but at the same time it's far from obvious.

When we consider any phenomenon, that is to say, a certain part of reality, be it a business or anything else for that matter, our mind creates a representation of that what we're trying to understand. The first step towards a representation is to break up the phenomenon into aspects and components. A totality of aspects and components is a structure.

The structure itself should comply with the famous MECE principle, brought into life by McKinsey & Company. Pronounced "me-see", it's a grouping principle for separating a set of items into subsets that are mutually exclusive and collectively exhaustive. The MECE principle is logically obvious and extremely effective in the business-mapping processes, because it facilitates the optimum arrangement of available information into a clear and comprehensive structure.

The second step is to understand the connectivity between the components, and the relationships between various aspects of the structure. It's like putting it up together into one whole, but only after it was decomposed into parts on the first step. This interconnected structure is called a framework. This is the same whole we had before the first step, yet this representation of the whole is on an entirely new level.

Depending on the case, we may choose an existing framework, customized for your company. Alternatively, if you have something truly unique, a framework can be built from ground zero.

A pre-existing framework may be of a general nature. Or it may be industry-specific. Or it may be company-specific. Or it may be specific to your vision.

The third step is to understand how this framework works, that is to say, how it evolves over time. It is in effect a living and breathing entity. On this level of understanding it's called a model. The model is a representation of the reality in our minds. A good model can explain the past. A really good model can also predict the future.

The fourth step is to formulate a hypothesis, which basically means to use the model to make a prediction about the consequences of a certain intervention, which is presumably leading to the desired results, which in our situation means whatever business objective we want to achieve.

The fifth step is to design a course of action around the hypothesis, to plan out the intervention which will take us to the desired results. This course of action, including why, what, how, and when, step by step, is called a strategy, which here is used in a wider sense of the term. It may be more precise to call it The Strategy and Implementation Plan.

A strategy is not guesswork, and it's never arbitrary. It's based on our understanding, which means developing the structure, the framework, and the model first.

What if a strategy doesn't work? That is to say, the strategy has been implemented, but the desired results haven't been achieved?

Well, it's not that the strategy doesn't work. It rather means that our model is reflecting the reality incorrectly, or our hypothesis is false, or our framework doesn't depict the right relationships, or our structure is missing some aspects or components. In other words, the strategy is always correct in relevance to the model, it's just that the model itself may not represent the reality adequately, and needs to be fine-tuned.

When done in practice, you can hardly notice five distinct steps. And if you don't know what to look for, the chances are you will miss the model altogether.

You'll surely notice the final step, the strategy, in case it's a strategy that's explicitly presented to you.

If this is the case, here is the problem:

On an aesthetic dimension, you'll miss appreciation of the beauty.

On a practical dimension, you'll perceive the strategy as an arbitrary course of action. Even if you go for it, you'll lack a sense of ownership, as well as motivation and confidence, being on the lookout for whom to blame if it doesn't work as desired.

That's why I discourage delivering a strategy in the form of advice.

Let me clarify.

As a CEO, before making a decision, you must understand how the strategy is emerging from the model. You must understand the model, even if not on a detailed level. In fact, within the model, the strategy must be almost obvious to you.

It shouldn't be presented to you as a recommendation. It should rather be a "picture" which gives you clarity and empowers you to make an intelligent decision.

True, the details and complexities may be numerous, but in the end, once developed and made explicit, the structure, the framework, the model, the hypothesis, and the strategy are usually simple, if not obvious.

Let me show you the process developed and extensively used by McKinsey & Company, and how it fits into what we've just described. Here are the steps in the process the way they've practiced it:

1. Framework, structure.
2. Hypothesis.
3. Facts.
4. Interpretation, meaning.
5. Recommendation.

They seem to use the terms framework and structure interchangeably, so overall, they don't distinguish between a structure, a framework, and a model. Such a simplified approach has its advantages, as it's better-suited for an untrained mind, yet, in my eyes it lacks clarity.

The end result, the deliverable in their scheme is "recommendation". I believe that this is much more than imprecision. This perception of the end result is a root of the troubles experienced by some companies which were involved in the process, as well as the negativity attributed to McKinsey & Company.

When a recommendation is given to a CEO, a CEO is facing a "Yes" or "No" decision. "Should I go for it, or should I not? Should I believe you, or should I not?" The kind of a question that calls for such a Yes-or-No answer is already flawed, as shown and explained in depth by Chip & Dan Heath. But besides being flawed, even if the recommendation is substantiated by a compelling presentation, the ownership of the decision and the sense of responsibility for it become diluted.

Instead, the end result of the process should be a compelling model. A CEO doesn't have to, but may want to look into the structure, the framework, and at various possible interventions. Regardless, the resulting model is simple and clear, and the options are transparent. The intervention and the strategy, and their variations, are emerging from the model and, in a sense, are obvious. A CEO is now equipped to make an intelligent decision and to comfortably and fully own the decision and the responsibility for the consequences.

Now let me explain two crucial and brilliant points in the approach which were arguably pioneered by McKinsey & Company, at least in the business world, and at least in using them explicitly and consistently.

First, the place of the facts and data.

Data gathering, discovering facts, conducting research, deciding on what data is relevant and meaningful - all this is a vast area in its own right, but what's of essence in our consideration here is that you never begin with facts and data. That would be counterproductive. You always build the model first.

Once the model is ready, only then ought you to bring the facts and the data INTO the model. There is no unstructured pile of data. Each fact is thus classified, and has its place in the structure.

Second, the nature of the process.

The process parallels the scientific methodology, the way science advances. The model and the hypothesis are introduced based on the data available in the past. The predictions are made, and the new data has been collected. If the predictions hold true, the model and the hypothesis are tentatively considered correct. If not - a new cycle begins.

In our case, in the world of business, when the strategy doesn't produce the desired results, before anything else, we acknowledge that this is normal. This is the risk and the uncertainty of the entrepreneurship in action. We simply reevaluate and fine-tune our approach. It may call for a minor change, or for a major restructuring.

"When the facts change, I change my mind. What do YOU do, sir?"

So, what could possibly require fine-tuning?

Well, we've got the components which comprise our structure, the relationships which unite our framework, the dynamics that explain how our system evolves over time, and hypothesis which predicts the consequences of our intervention, with a step-by-step course of action which is designed to implement the hypothesis in real life.

This is what we have, and this is what we fine-tune. It's up to specifics. Nothing more can be said in general.

EXECUTIVE SUMMARY.

Let's put it all together:

→ You understand and describe your industry in terms of its definitive forces: customers, their needs, substitutes, partners and suppliers, competitors, entry barriers, access and consumption.

→ You formulate your competitive strategy (4 ingredients plus a definitive idea).

→ The competitive strategy provides the competitive advantage that allows the customer to discover your company and choose your products and services among many other solutions in the market.

→ You develop a model of your business based on the value chain which is designed to support and execute your competitive strategy. The value chain is represented by a series of distinctions allowing you to group and classify all your business activities, as well as quantify them by measuring their impact on your bottom line, which usually implies profitability and shareholder value.

→ As you move forward by developing, implementing, and skillfully executing your competitive strategy, you set and achieve the milestones; you solve the problems and overcome the challenges you encounter, by designing, implementing, and executing the appropriate strategies.

→ From a bird's-eye view the overall process is as follows:

◆ The model and the hypothesis are introduced based on interpretation of the available data, combined with intuition.

◆ Possible interventions are considered, the hypothesis is clearly defined, the primary intervention is chosen, the predictions are made, and the strategy is designed and executed.

◆ The new data is collected. If the predictions hold true and the desired results have been achieved, the model and the hypothesis are tentatively considered correct and further interventions are planned and implemented based on this model. If not - a new cycle begins, i.e. the model is fine-tuned, and a new hypothesis is introduced, etc.

Understanding and applying this conceptual framework for your business gives you an enormous advantage, and is the key to superior economic performance and profitability.

The 10-point strategy conceptual framework in a nutshell:

- 1. The industry forces & The Competitive **Strategy** (the 4 ingredients and the definitive idea).
- 2. Competitive **advantage**
  - 3. **Executing** competitive strategy and achieving a competitive advantage.
    - 4. **Value chain** (model)
    - 5. Classifying, grouping, and quantifying business **activities**
    - 6. **Milestones**
      - 7. **Problems**
      - 8. **Objectives**
    - 9. **Strategies** (solving problems and meeting objectives)
      - 10. **Executing** the strategies

The <u>process</u> in a nutshell:

- Model -> Hypothesis -> Facts -> Strategy -> Execution -> [repeat]
  - Structure - Framework - [Draft] Model
  - Facts & data
  - Hypothesis -> Intervention [options] -> Interpretation, meaning -> [Final] Model -> The intervention [chosen] -> Strategy -> Execute
    - Repeat

CHAPTER 7

The Position of a CEO: Selected Highlights

Seven responsibilities of a CEO

1. Creating, communicating, and implementing the organization's vision, mission, and overall direction.

2. Leading the development and implementation of the organization's strategy.

3. Acquisition, organization, and allocation of the human, physical, and financial capital.

4. Assessing the principal risks of the organization and ensuring that these risks are monitored and managed.

5. Leading, guiding, directing, and evaluating the work of other executives.

6. Overseeing the complete operation of an organization in accordance with the strategic plans.

7. Evaluating the success of the organization in reaching its goals.

Briefly:

1. **Vision** - creating, communicating.

2. **Strategy** - development, implementation.

3. **Capital** - organization, allocation and management.

4. **Risks** - monitor, manage.

5. **Leading** - executives.

6. **Overseeing** - operations.

7. **Success** - evaluating.

Four functional levels:

- **Entrepreneurship** - risking the capital.

- **CEO** - strategies (designing a master plan, selecting and strategizing opportunities, managing the risks, coordinating resources).

- **Executives** - coordinating the workforce.

- **Workforce** - implementing the strategies.

On Leadership

Kabbalah describes ten spiritual forces that have been employed in creating and managing everything in existence. The lowest of the ten is called Kingship. This is surprising: isn't kingship about reigning above, being in control, imposing the will on those below? How can kingship be the lowest of all?

The deepest wisdom of a great kingdom is that a king has nothing on his own. A king is surrounded by talents, brilliance, and the strengths of others, and is able to unite and channel all the energies. It's the humblest position to be in: you have nothing of your own. At the same time, it's the most powerful position to be in: you channel great energies and facilitate great impact in the world.

It's like being a moon, reflecting the sun's light. A moon doesn't envy the sun's energy, does it? It just reflects it humbly, being fully satisfied with such a "secondary" role.

A modern term for kingship is leadership. A leader is not a benevolent dictator. A leader has the rare quality of being surrounded by brilliance and talent, uniting the energies, and channeling them to create an impact in the world.

Leadership is a very humble position to be in. A leader transmits the powerful lights, yet doesn't own them. Others do, it's their talents, their energy, their dedication.

The inherent greatness of a CEO is in being humble, in developing other people, in focusing on other people's strengths and enjoying their growth and success.

If you're asked to ascribe two qualities, brilliance and loyalty, to a CEO and those under the CEO's command, how would you do it?

Most people would ascribe brilliance to a CEO and loyalty to others. A brilliant CEO is leading a loyal team.

A paradoxical truth is that it's the other way around: in the ideal organization, the team members are brilliant, each one with his or her own brilliance, while the CEO is loyal to the team and dedicated to developing their talents even further. The more brilliant, accomplished, successful they are, the happier the CEO is.

On A Whole

We can now notice one more ingredient here. This ingredient is hidden, yet crucial. Let's call this ingredient ONENESS: it means keeping a whole, not allowing any part of the organization to disrupt its wholesomeness.

This concerns all the parts and aspects of the organization, but this is especially challenging when it comes to people. They are all brilliant and talented. How do you keep them as a whole?

The only way a conflict doesn't destroy a whole is enclosing a conflict in a larger context, which by itself is fully compatible with the opposite opinions.

How so?

Let's say we disagree on A and B.

Before we try to reconcile our disagreement, let's find a perspective C, which is higher than A and B. In fact, C includes elements of A and B in a way, such that we would fully agree on C, while still disagreeing on A and B. More specifically, we both agree that we need to reach C; we're rather arguing on the way to achieve C - either through A, or through B.

The larger context should also be infused with a warmer relationship which transcends the conflict per se. The warmth of the relationship and the common goals drastically change the game.

This is how a disagreement is enveloped into an agreement, and becomes constructive and easier to handle.

When a conflict is handled this way, it nurtures and strengthens a whole, instead of disrupting and breaking it apart.

It's one of the greatest challenges of a CEO to maintain the organization as a WHOLE in ALL its parts and aspects. Each piece, each individual, each conflict is a part of a whole and is rather enhancing and strengthening the organization, instead of fragmenting it.

The concept of a whole and its application to the organization is important on a daily basis. Whether explicit or implicit, each decision, each choice must preserve the whole of the company. While ROI considerations are always critical, preserving and developing the whole is no less important!

But what is a whole, in practical terms?

Well, the whole arises from your mission, vision, direction, definition. You have to define your company, your value, your contribution and impact. This is a conversation you want to have BEFORE you go on and make important decisions. It may sound vague, and it is vague on an abstract level, but once we get to the specifics of your company, the vagueness shapes up and crystallizes, and the nebulous whole gradually appears in your vision and becomes very tangible.

On Financing

This is almost obvious, yet worth rehearsing.

An opportunity always has the risks and the benefits associated with it. In allocating the capital for the opportunity, you're risking the capital, hopefully, in a managed, controlled manner, and you target actualizing the benefits.

What if an opportunity is good and the risk is small, but you don't have a necessary investment? Should you finance it or not?

Let's consider an example.

A 17-year-old works hard 50 hours a week for $10 an hour and health benefits. $2,000 monthly salary in total, $1,500 a month is spent on basic necessities, $500 is saved.

It takes 400 months to save $200,000 (33 years and 4 months).

By the age of 50 (17+33), one saves $200,000 and is now ready to go to a medical school. Fast-forward another 9 years, by the age of 59, one becomes a doctor. Let's assume he spends another year resting a bit, looking for a job, and finally at the age of 60 begins a career as a doctor.

Let's consider an alternative scenario. If our 17-year-old borrows $200,000 to pay for the medical school, and becomes a doctor in 9 years, by the age of 26, assuming the doctor's annual salary is $200,000 and $100,000 is spent on basic and not-so-basic necessities, with

$100,000 a year used to pay back the loan, let's review the immense difference.

- 33 years and 4 months spent to earn the medical school costs, **against** 2 years with the same result.

- $1,500 monthly allowance **against** $100,000 annual allowance.

Well, we didn't consider taxes, interest, and a few more details, but details don't matter. You've got the point: financing opportunities is a powerful amplifier. When an opportunity is really good, it may be worth financing. If an opportunity is not so good, then either skip it altogether, or spend only what you have, as it's not worth financing.

Evaluating opportunities becomes critical. If you have a budget for one opportunity only, you still can pursue ten opportunities if you choose to finance them. Of course, they'd better be good, but they don't ALL have to be successful for your business to succeed overall! Even SOME opportunities resulting in success may mean wild success for your business as a whole.

On Opportunities

What's the essential difference between a successful $1 million business, a successful $10 million business, and a successful $100 million business?

$1 million business: you perceived an opportunity and risked the capital to generate the value to satisfy the market's needs. You were correct in your assumption. It was still risky, but you won: the market responded and readily consumed the $1 million value.

There are ways to amplify the $1 million success and take it to $10+ million if the market allows it, but a $100 million business is of a different nature.

A $100 million business is built around multiple opportunities, taken one after another, in a series of entrepreneurial endeavors.

In a sense, a $1 million business CEO is an occasional entrepreneur, while a $100 million business CEO is a lifestyle and serial entrepreneur, by being entrepreneurial again and again within one very company.

You don't always have to grow. You may be perfectly fine where you are, by capitalizing on the opportunity you discovered and built a while ago. But if you really want to grow, you need to become entrepreneurial again, and be on the lookout for new opportunities under the umbrella of your business.

Last but not least, evaluating an opportunity from a ROI point of view is, of course, a must, yet evaluating an opportunity from a WHOLE point of view is no less important! You have to be aware how exactly an opportunity strengthens and enhances your business as a whole. You have to make sure that an opportunity does NOT fragment your business by breaking it apart just because the numbers seem to look good.

On a larger scale, when it comes to new opportunities, there are three types of analysis you are to conduct: RISK-analysis, ROI-analysis, and WHOLE-analysis.

An opportunity may sound appealing, yet an opportunity contains the risks and the responsibilities. Opportunities are not to be taken lightly...

CHAPTER 8

Leadership Labs

A s we've stated earlier, "Leadership is a very humble position to be in. A leader transmits the powerful lights, yet doesn't own them. Others do; it's their talents, their energy, their dedication. The inherent greatness of a CEO is in being humble, in developing other people, in focusing on other people's strengths and enjoying their growth and success."

There are two key terms that express the essence of leadership:

1. Focus

2. Channeling

Focus implies vision, long-term and short-term vision. You can't focus without having a vision to focus ON. A leader develops a high-level vision.

Channeling is more abstract. What does it mean exactly? What does channeling imply, practically speaking? A great concept, yet what do you DO? How does it look and feel, hands-on, to be humble and "reflect the light of others"?

Let's bring the beautiful and powerful concept down to earth, at least in one of its aspects.

Originally developed and described comprehensively by Chet Holmes, when employed consistently, this will inevitably take your business, your company to an entirely new level.

The foundation is to understand what you, as a leader, bring to the table, and what others, those who are led by you, bring.

Forget the headache of hunting for problems, digging for solutions, trying to figure out what to achieve and how. You don't have to do any of those.

You bring YOUR JUDGMENT. You don't have to bring anything else. Sure, you may, if it comes your way, but you don't necessarily have to. In fact, if you do bring something else, do it AS IF it's somebody else who does it. Yours is only a judgment, that's all.

Still too abstract?

Here is an example (well, it's much more than an example; this is a simple change with the most profound impact, despite its simplicity):

Establish regular workshop-style meetings dedicated to improving every aspect of your business. Each meeting is focusing on just one small part of the business.

Pose a question or propose a subject for the meeting.

You don't have to think hard to come up with a question or a subject. You only need one main agenda per meeting, and here are some examples:

- "What are our three biggest problems?"
- "What are the three things that we can improve?"
- "What is the biggest obstacle that holds you back in terms of your performance and results?"
- "What else can we offer to our customers at a point of sale?"
- "How do we implement this for us?"
- "How do we apply this idea to us?"
- "How do we fish for ideas that will help us transform and grow as a business?"
- "What's the biggest frustration in your job?"

A question or a subject can be very general, or very specific.

You can pose a question or a problem, or an issue, or a suggestion, or an idea, or a solution, or anything else in the world. You can pose a request to come up with problems, issues, suggestions, ideas, and solutions, in case you're not sure what's the most important at the moment or what would be the most beneficial.

Let others do the work! Let others accomplish! Let others make a difference!

Conduct a meeting by engaging your people. Remember, the conductor of an orchestra doesn't make a sound! Your people will come up with more options and ideas than you could possibly imagine.

Write down all the options on the board. Arrange a vote to assign a priority level for each item on the list. This is how you create a master list of all your company's problems (or department's, or whatever unit of the company it's applicable to) and prioritize them.

If you dedicate a meeting to a problem, don't jump to a solution too quickly. Explore the problem domain comprehensively first, with your team's help.

Let me remind you: you bring your judgment, and, in addition, a reflection on everything that transpires during the meeting. You will register and analyze, and later you will decide what to focus on further, so you will have a few decisions to make on the way, but even the decisions will often be based on voting, unless you have a compelling reason to use your authority to overrule an opinion of the majority (and whenever it happens - explain!).

Let's take a step back. From a bird's eye view, here is the structure of the experience, where each line loosely corresponds to a separate meeting, or at least a distinct segment of the meeting:

- Which objective to pursue?
    - Why to pursue this objective and not another one?
    - How exactly to pursue this objective?
        - What's the plan or the strategy to meet the objective?

- What are the obstacles to overcome in order to implement the strategy efficiently and effectively?
- What is the next obstacle to tackle?
- Who is doing what - setting assignments.
- Who has done what - reviewing the results; analyzing, fine-tuning, deciding on a next step.
  - Celebrating the victories, as well as learning valuable lessons from failures.
  - Celebrating the winners - recognition of the impact of your people is of paramount importance.

If the objective is unclear, begin from the objective. If the objective is clear, begin from the obstacles. If the obstacles are clear, jump to solutions.

This is what generally transpires, whether you consider an objective or an obstacle, and anything else for that matter:

- An unordered Master List of items (achieved by the team's brainstorming).
- An orderly Master List of items (the order is based on voting and/or given priorities).
- For each item in the Master List:
  - Focus on the item.
    - Come up with a list of options (on how to address the item; brainstorming by the team).
    - Select an option to pursue.
    - Assign a chosen option to those who will execute it.
- Document every step on the way. Document every meeting. Reflect on what transpired and understand it well.
- Remember: yours is a judgment; you're NOT responsible for input or output. You welcome, focus, and channel the ideas of others, the work of others, the energy of others.

Each meeting deserves a summary of its own. Often times, even more than a summary. Document everything as you go. Spell out every step.

A corresponding memo is created and broadcasted. As time goes by, a collection of the memos will be transformed into the training manual. As time goes by further, you will create policies, based on the training manual.

There will be at least fifty memos per year, as the meetings are conducted weekly. Accordingly, the training manual and the best policies will grow and acquire structure.

It's really that simple:

- Pose a question.

- Encourage engagement.

- Let the energies flow.

- Gently direct, focus, channel, crystallize, reflect, capture.

It's not about you. Let others come up with issues and problems, and let others solve them all too.

Depending on the size of your company, it may concern the whole company (all the employees at once), or one branch at a time, or a department, or a team, or only the executives, or only employees with a certain function, or any other unit of the company. Accordingly, this may be done by a CEO, by any other executive, by a manager, or by a supervisor – it all depends on what's reasonable for the size of your company and for the team involved. In fact, these weekly meetings should ideally be conducted on every level of the company.

Together you will brainstorm ideas for how to improve any specific area, draft procedures to test, and ultimately create company policies that everyone will be trained to follow.

Gradually the systems will be designed, developed, and installed. To reiterate, your main contribution is the overall framework and your judgment. In a sense, you don't have to have anything on your own. Of course, you may, but it's unnecessary. Your role is humble indeed: focus others, engage others, let them shine, and channel their energies.

This is how your team will be empowered and your people will perform "magic". These kinds of "simple" weekly meetings will magically take you to the next level. You can't possibly predict the results and the impact, as this will stimulate your team's energies way beyond your personal abilities and even imagination.

By following the process consistently, you will discover powerful solutions to the problems you were aware of, and to those you were unaware of. Implementing the solutions might not be easy though, because humans are naturally averse to change, especially major and sudden change, and also because small incremental improvements are easy to overlook and hard to appreciate.

The key to successful implementation, besides being persistent, is showing your team the consequences. The painful consequences of maintaining the status quo, and the glorious consequences of having solutions in place.

Even when consequences are self-evident, people are rarely consciously aware of them. Our minds are "lazy" in perceiving implications. That's why you always need to amplify the painful consequences in people's minds, as well as intensify the victory and the accomplishment. Your ability to show implications and stir emotions is directly proportional to your success in implementing changes throughout your company.

Also, as a rule, begin implementing any changes from your best people, from your champions and star performers. Watch them closely, measure, capture, and document. You will use these case studies internally in your organization as a proof of concept, as a guide, and as motivation and inspiration for others. This is a hidden secret that makes a difference between success and failure in implementing ideas, innovations, and making changes last, when other people are involved.

CHAPTER 9

The Sales & Marketing Toolbox

As highlighted earlier, from the very inception of a business, the primary attention and energies of a CEO should be focused on marketing and sales. With the growth of the company to a certain size or level, the CEO gradually transitions to the main function of capital allocation, while the functions of marketing and sales are delegated to the executives under him.

In this sense therefore, before the turning point, marketing and sales are pivotal functions of a CEO, hence we're going to cover these areas comprehensively, by developing the sales and marketing toolbox.

Before introducing and explaining the toolbox, we'll go over four foundational concepts whose importance cannot be overestimated.

- Foundational Four Concepts
  - Online World
  - Offer Flexibility
  - Follow-up
  - The Scientific Method & its application to business

- The Sales & Marketing Toolbox
  - 10 Instruments
    - Toolbox brief
    - Toolbox detailed
    - Toolbox explained

Online World

The internet and the online world have drastically redefined humanity and the way we communicate. Your clients and customers are no longer the same. This is why more companies are increasingly becoming frustrated with their marketing and customer-acquisition strategies and results.

Have you adjusted your marketing and sales processes accordingly?

❖ "My clients are not online."

❖ "My clients can't be attracted online."

❖ "My services can't be sold online."

❖ "I've tried online marketing. Nothing worked."

❖ "Online? Not for my clients."

First of all, YOUR clients ARE online:

➢ Google: **1,800,000,000** Estimated Unique Monthly Visitors

➢ Bing: **500,000,000** Estimated Unique Monthly Visitors

➢ Yahoo! Search: **490,000,000** Estimated Unique Monthly Visitors

➢ Baidu: **480,000,000** Estimated Unique Monthly Visitors

➢ Ask: **300,000,000** Estimated Unique Monthly Visitors

➢ AOL Search: **200,000,000** Estimated Unique Monthly Visitors

➢ DuckDuckGo: **150,000,000** Estimated Unique Monthly Visitors

➢ WolframAlpha: **35,000,000** Estimated Unique Monthly Visitors

- Yandex: **30,000,000** Estimated Unique Monthly Visitors

- WebCrawler: **25,000,000** Estimated Unique Monthly Visitors

- Search: **20,000,000** Estimated Unique Monthly Visitors

- Dogpile: **12,000,000** Estimated Unique Monthly Visitors

- Ixquick: **11,000,000** Estimated Unique Monthly Visitors

- Excite: **8,000,000** Estimated Unique Monthly Visitors

- Info: **7,000,000** Estimated Unique Monthly Visitors

- Total monthly searches: over **4,000,000,000 (4 BILLION)**

- Total social media users: about **2,500,000,000 (2.5 BILLION)**

- Total online users: over **7,500,000,000 (7.5 BILLION)**

It may be not immediately apparent WHERE your prospective clients are online, or what exactly they are doing online, but THEY ARE ONLINE, whoever they are, whatever they are.

Once they are online, assuming you know where they are, what they are doing there and why, you CAN attract their attention, even if for a brief moment.

The next challenge is to figure out what to tell them during that fraction of a second when you're holding their attention. Obviously, immediately offering them your service or product is usually a waste of time, and so too is telling them about your company or accomplishments. You have to learn to become more flexible than that. Hence the next section, which we call OFFER FLEXIBILITY.

Please note: In our context, the online world as a concept does not simply imply online internet platforms only. It rather implies inclusion of the holistic online universe, as an integral part of experience for almost every human being. Online and offline are two parts of the same whole, and the borderline is hardly visible, as our online and offline experiences are synergistically merged in our lives.

Offer Flexibility

The term "offer flexibility" is mine, but the best explanation and hands-on approach arguably belongs to Chet Holmes:

Your audience can be divided into five categories in relation to your direct offer:

➤ 3% Buying now

➤ 7% Open to it

➤ 30% Not thinking about it

➤ 30% Thinking they are not interested

➤ 30% Definitely NOT interested

Once you begin talking about your offer, or even your company, you immediately lose 97% of the audience. The remaining 3% is not a free lunch either. It's going to be tough.

Now let's change the game. Forget about your service, your product, and your company altogether.

Imagine you're selling a legal research tool to large law firms. The executives refuse to talk to you, they send you to librarians. The librarians love your tool, but can't write a check, and can't sell your tool for you to the executives either.

Solution?

You're no longer selling anything. You contact the partners, and here are the excerpts from your conversations with them (quoting Chet Holmes):

- *"We've been helping <u>law firms</u> be more successful for more than 15 years. We recently commissioned a study on what's going on in the <u>legal market</u> and we've learned that there are some pretty serious challenges facing <u>lawyers</u> in the new millennium."*

- *"Since our survival depends on your success, we wanted to make sure that you saw this information, and had every opportunity to be ahead of the problems. We put this information into a very succinct executive committee orientation and we're now showing this to all the top <u>law firms</u>. In fact, we're in touch with [company A company B company C,] and we're in a process of arranging to show this in their management meetings. We want to make sure you also saw this very important information."*

- *"$3 million worth of raw data that we condensed and put in a format that's designed to be fast-paced, easy to grasp, and highly educational."*

- *"90% of what I am going to cover is educational in nature and designed to serve you. At the end, we have a little PR section about us, which is kind of to let you know about what's going on with us, if you're interested. And if you're not interested, we can just skip that part. Does that seem fair?"*

- *"What's in it for you?"*, they ask you.
  - You answer, *"Well, it's a public relations effort for our company, a way of getting in front of more people like yourself, it's a way of learning more about the industry, and it's the way to give back. Plus, we're dependent on this industry to be successful, so we want to make sure that people like you have the best information possible."*

As you've noticed, it's a totally different conversation. The focus is shifted from your company, product or service, to their world:

> "5 most dangerous trends facing manufacturers"

> "4 most dangerous trends facing law firms"

> "3 most dangerous trends facing the insurance industry"

> "Ordinary problems & extraordinary solutions in the roofing industry today"

In fact, I personally used the last line ("Ordinary problems & extraordinary solutions in the roofing industry today"), and after spending $656.81 on Facebook got 351 clicks, of whom 9 people gave out their contact information and asked me to call them. 6 of the 9 were CEOs of $25+ million roofing companies. This was my first experiment attracting executives of such a caliber. I was told that it was a mission impossible, and I believed it was probably true, but I decided to try just in case. The results shocked me at the time.

There is more to this approach, but the point is not to show you the whole system now. The point is that if you become creative and flexible, and look way beyond your direct offer, you can have meaningful, impactful, and far-reaching conversations with your potential clients which you wouldn't be able to otherwise.

Let's have a look at your audience again:

- ➢ 3% Buying now

- ➢ 7% Open to it

- ➢ 30% Not thinking about it

- ➢ 30% Thinking they are not interested

- ➢ 30% Definitely NOT interested

With the "flexible offer", ALL 100% are suddenly interested, and it's no longer as tough, even with the 30% who are definitely not interested in your product or service YET.

Why?

You are looking to give, to serve - NOT to take, to sell.

"Flexible offers" work wonders online and offline. They change your marketing and sales experience once and forever.

Follow-up

Only 2% of all sales are made on the first contact.

Another 3% of sales are made on the second contact.

80% of all sales are made between 5 and 12 contacts.

According to the statistics, the single biggest opportunity in sales is FOLLOW-UP. It's as simple as that.

However, massive, systematic, and consistent follow-up is not that simple. Planning, enforcing, and automating follow-up is the science and the art.

There are many ways to follow up, depending on the circumstances:

- SMS or text messaging
- Email
- Handwritten notes
- Personal visit
- Voice message
- Ringless message drops
- Hand-delivered packages
- FedExed packages

How many times should you follow-up?

Here is a follow-up schedule from Ryan Stewman:

- 5 minutes after the conversation
- 1st day after the conversation
- 2nd day
- 3rd day
- 4th day
- 5th day
- 10th day
- 14th day
- 21st day
- 30th day
- 40th day
- 50th day
- 60th day
- 75th day

- 90th day
- 100th day
- 120th day
- 150th day
- 180th day
- 210th day
- 240th day
- 270th day
- 300th day
- 330th day
- 365th day (with the note "We are not going away! It's been one year! We're having our anniversary!")

Of course, sometimes such a follow-up may be inappropriate, especially for high-ticket professional services, but once a week, or once in two weeks, or once a month may always be appropriate and very effective in all cases – especially when approached with creativity and fun, and combined with the "flexible offer" idea. There is nobody in the world you can't possibly attract with a proper follow-up.

The beauty of the follow-up concept is that you don't have to have a full-fledged interaction before you begin follow-up. If you just send an email, a letter, or a package, you can - and you should - follow-up! This is how follow-up becomes a powerful strategy of approaching and developing relationships with virtually anyone.

The Scientific Method - and its application to business

This is how the scientific method is used in science:

- The scientific method is a continuous process that begins with **observations**.
- Reflecting on observations, we develop ideas or **hypotheses** about why things are the way they are.
- The best hypotheses lead to **predictions** that must be tested. The purpose of a test is to determine whether observations

agree with or conflict with the predictions derived from a hypothesis. **Testing** is an investigation of whether the real world behaves as predicted by the hypothesis.

- We test hypotheses by conducting **experiments**. The purpose of an experiment is to determine whether observations of the real world agree with or conflict with the predictions derived from a hypothesis. If they agree, confidence in the hypothesis increases; otherwise, it decreases. However, agreement does not assure that the hypothesis is true; future experiments may reveal problems.

- **Analysis** involves determining what the results of the experiment show and deciding on the next actions to take.

- If the evidence has falsified the hypothesis, a new hypothesis is required; if the experiment supports the hypothesis but the evidence is not strong enough for high confidence, other predictions from the hypothesis must be tested. Once a hypothesis is strongly supported by evidence, a new question can be asked to provide further insight on the same topic. A new question may introduce new distinctions, or a new dimension of the area in consideration.

- Depending on how well experiments match the predictions, the original hypothesis may require refinement, alteration, expansion, or rejection.

- If a particular hypothesis becomes very well-supported, a general theory, or a **model**, may be developed. When a hypothesis is introduced, the theory or the model is already implied. In fact, the hypothesis itself may be derived from a tentative model, and in this sense, the process begins with a model. However, the model is not developed fully and clearly until the hypothesis is confirmed with a certain level of confidence.

The scientific method applies to business in its entirety. Instead of nature and discovery of the secrets of nature, we have business and discovery of the secrets of profitability. These are the steps of the business development and optimization process, a blueprint of taking a business opportunity from conception to life and success:

- Observations
- Tentative model
- Hypotheses
- Predictions
- Testing: experiments
- Analysis
- Evidence - hypotheses requires:
  - refinement,
  - alteration,
  - expansion,
  - or rejection.
- Repetition - a number of iterations.
- The Model is kept, and understood deeper and clearer.

Correspondingly, any marketing or sales project consists of an initial, sometimes even partial, build and setup. This is followed by an iterative process: developing, fine-tuning, and optimizing, first making it work, and then making it work better. We go through iterations, until the objectives are met, thus embracing the opportunity, or until we can't keep investing in the process until the objectives are met, thus rejecting the opportunity.

The Sales & Marketing Toolbox

As you can expect, a toolbox is a collection of tools. But let's not take the terms for granted. What does "a tool" mean in the context of marketing and sales?

"A tool" is a very important concept. Understanding it clearly will have profound implications for your business.

A tool is a distinctive factor. Distinctions slice up the wealth of phenomena of marketing and sales, allowing us to laser-focus on a specific part or aspect, effectively shedding a new light so that we see things in a way we haven't seen before, which in turn enables us to develop specific strategies rooted in this new view of business phenomena.

As you can expect from a collection of tools, it conforms to the MECE principle which we've already discussed: the collection is mutually exclusive and collectively exhaustive. This practically means that ALL your sales and marketing activities and strategies can be derived from the toolbox. Even though further distinctions can be made when necessary, there is nothing really beyond the toolbox.

Interestingly, a distinction itself may be simple, almost commonsensical. Furthermore, with the right distinction, a set of strategies often becomes a matter of common sense too. However, when the common sense is compounded from one step to another, the resulting strategies contain a degree of novelty, as they are not as easily apparent before the distinction is applied.

A toolbox is a set of such distinctions, where each one sheds a new light on the area of marketing and sales, and leads to a series of powerful strategies.

Warning: taken as a whole, the toolbox is overwhelming and unmanageable. However, the power and the beauty of the distinctions manifests when you take one distinction at a time, focus on it, and view the subject matter through the light of the distinction. Everything suddenly becomes simple, if not obvious, and the ideas and the strategies appear, develop, and crystallize quickly.

The following three sections are: 1) toolbox brief, 2) toolbox detailed, 3) toolbox explained.

If this is the first time you're reading this, please jump to the 3rd section right away. The first two sections, toolbox brief and toolbox detailed, won't tell you much without reading the 3rd section first. "Toolbox brief" is a collection of all ten tools (distinctions). "Toolbox detailed" is a detailed view, where each tool is broken down into further distinctions, to make it more specific, practical, and easy to apply. The first two sections are meant to be a refresher, a reference, a table of content, and an idea generator AFTER you've become familiar with the material explained in the 3rd section, named "toolbox explained".

Toolbox Brief

1. More leads
2. More conversions
3. More offers
4. Re-igniting leads
5. Re-igniting customers
6. More referrals
7. Better offers
8. More salespeople
9. Better salespeople
10. Leverage & multiply

Toolbox Detailed

1. More leads
   a. Communication channels
      i. Online
         1. Search-based
         2. Display-based
         3. Identity-based
      ii. By email
      iii. By phone
      iv. By mail
   b. Targeting options
      i. 1-on-1
      ii. A few
      iii. A lot
2. More conversions
   a. Conversion optimization process

   i. Measuring everything

   ii. Fine-tuning the funnel [steps]

  b. Massive, systematic, consistent follow-up

3. More Offers

  a. Same

   i. The same offer - offering more often

  b. Horizontal

   i. Other relevant offers - complementing the main offer

  c. Vertical

   i. Spectrum of value - less or more value - minimizing and maximizing the value of the main offer

4. Re-igniting leads (reactivating leads acquired earlier, those who didn't convert)

  a. Online world

  b. Offer flexibility

  c. Scientific method

  d. Follow-up

5. Re-igniting customers (reactivating customers acquired earlier, i.e. those who converted)

  a. Online world

  b. Offer flexibility

  c. Scientific method

  d. Follow-up

6. More referrals

  a. Online world

  b. Offer flexibility

  c. Scientific method

  d. Follow-up

7. Better offers

  a. Less selfish, more altruistic - taking less, giving more

  b. Giving value without taking anything at all - purely altruistic

8. More salespeople

  a. An ad, an offer

  b. Pre-interview

  c. Interview

9. Better salespeople

   a. Regular meetings
       i.   Reviewing numbers
       ii. Reviewing techniques
       iii. Reviewing difficulties
       iv. Aha-moments
   b. Trainings, workshops, demonstrations, etc.
   c. Replicating success
       i.   Capturing
       ii. Understanding, reviewing
       iii. Sharing

10. Leverage & multiply
   a. Script
   b. Automate
       i.   Gradual building by extension and expansion
   c. Conversion optimization process
   d. Common mistakes:
       i.   Mass marketing and sales is not preceded by 1-on-1 approach
       ii. 1-on-1 marketing and sales is not followed by mass approach. 1-on-1 can always be scaled, leveraged, automated, etc.

Toolbox Explained

More Leads (tool #1)

The first distinction: focusing exclusively on acquiring new leads. How do we get them?

Introducing a further distinction: **communication channels**. There are four main communication channels we can employ to connect with the prospects:

Online.

      There are three types of online targeting: search-based, display-based, and identity-based. Generally, ANY of the three may be effective in generating the flow of leads for you.

Search-based:

> You are to discover what your potential clients are searching for, and where exactly. This may be subtle, as they may not necessarily search for your product or service directly.

Display-based:

> You're to discover what online information your potential clients consume, and where exactly. You can pick them up right from there. This may be subtle, as they may not necessarily consume information that directly correlates with your product or service.

Identity-based:

> You're to profile your potential clients. Any identity-related information may be useful and applied accordingly. There are many companies that provide advanced data services which allow you to target virtually ANY clients for ANY type of business based on their identity.

By email

By messenger

By phone

By mail

There are many ways to find the emails, the phone numbers, and mailing addresses of your potential prospects.

It's very powerful to combine various communication channels: email, phone, and mail, alternating them for the same very prospect.

It's also very important to realize that to implement the strategies successfully, you may need to apply **the foundational concepts** all the way through:

Online World.

Realize that your potential clients are members of the modern society, and ARE using ALL communication channels, and ARE reachable online, by email, by phone, and by mail, as well as in person, when appropriate.

Offer Flexibility.

By talking about yourself or your products and services, you effectively kill almost any opportunity to win prospective clients in the earlier stages. This is NOT because the opportunity is not there or something doesn't work. It is because you need to exercise greater flexibility in crafting your offers, as (conceptually) you have to become a giver and not taker, a trusted advisor and not a salesperson, value provider and not money taker; you have to be talking to your whole audience and not to a tiny reluctant minority, you need to establish and gradually develop relationship and not be transaction-oriented, etc.

Follow-up.

Always, always, always follow-up. Follow-up must be massive, systematic, and consistent. Follow-up is a strategy and requires your undivided attention, when appropriate. It's not enough to have an idea about the importance of follow-up. It's also not enough to simply know the statistics of the effectiveness of follow-up. Follow-up must be artfully orchestrated and implemented, enforced or automated when appropriate.

The Scientific Method.

Anything and everything in marketing and sales is based on certain assumptions, predictions, trial and error, and is iterative by nature. Nothing ever works right away! It usually makes sense to set aside a reasonable budget to test an idea or an opportunity. You budget time, effort, and money, and set the desired results. You test, and test, and test, first making it work, then making it work better, fine-tuning and optimizing, and once the forecasted budget is exhausted, either embrace the opportunity as an integral part of your system or discard it for good. There are very few opportunities in marketing and sales which take less than 3-4 months to test iteratively, and, depending on the situation, may take longer, or even much longer. But whatever it takes, it has to be planned and budgeted, so there will be no surprises.

Targeting options.

Whether you approach your prospects by email, on the phone, or by mail, you can target them 1-on-1, in small groups, or in larger groups:

1-on-1

There are commercial business databases available which allow you to pinpoint your best potential clients, one at a time. You can also pick your prospects from the news or business publications, online or offline, and apply follow-up strategy in combination with other foundational concepts we've already explained.

A few

A lot

Whether you work with your prospects dozens at a time, or hundreds at a time, or thousands at a time, there are many ways to get their contact information. There are many free and paid directories and databases, trade and professional associations, expo participants directories. An often-underestimated source is hiring data scrapers and data miners who are trained to traverse the deepest recesses of the Internet in search for your best prospects, as long as you provide some meaningful criteria to identify them.

More Conversions (tool #2)

We're no longer focusing on getting new leads. We're assuming that a healthy flow of leads is being generated, and now we want to convert more prospects into buyers. How do we do it?

The scientific method is meticulously applied to your business. You may call it a conversion optimization process, to use familiar terms.

Everything we said on the subject of scientific method when we discussed new leads applies here too. Our objective is increasing conversions, i.e. converting more prospects into clients. We make assumptions, build hypotheses and a model, and test it all out.

It's a tedious and iterative process, measuring everything, fine-tuning the process by fine-tuning the steps of the process, and, of course, massive, systematic and consistent follow-up. And never, never forget about the offer flexibility!

(Please note: It is beyond the scope of this book to show the blueprint of the system necessary to be in place in order to take a client from what we call "a flexible offer" to our direct offer, i.e. to our main product or service.)

More Offers (tool #3)

The more offers we make, the more sales result. It's as simple as that. However, there are some distinctions to make, as the matter is not trivial.

- Whatever offer we have, whether flexible or direct, we should make it more often in the ongoing follow-up communication.
- We can often complement our main offer, by offering other generally relevant offers that correlate with our main (or front-end) offer.
- For any offer, there is a whole spectrum of offers to consider, or, more precisely, a spectrum of value. We can minimize or maximize the included value, so the offer will change accordingly.
  As usual, our foundational concepts, online world, offer flexibility, follow-up, and scientific method, ALL apply here as well.

Re-Igniting Leads (tool #4)

(reactivating leads acquired earlier, those who didn't convert)

> This is as simple, or as complex, as the follow-up concept and strategy we've already covered. In a sense, it's a tool on its own. There is almost no such a thing as a lost or hopeless lead. Any lead can, and should be "warmed up" and brought closer to a sale.

> Our foundation, consisting of online world, offer flexibility, and scientific method fully applies here as usual.

Re-Igniting Customers (tool #5)

(reactivating customers acquired earlier, i.e. those who converted)

> This is again as simple, or as complex, as the follow-up concept and strategy. It's a different follow-up in comparison with re-igniting leads, but the difference is rather in the content, not in the form.

> Through a skillful follow-up, we're taking our existing or former customers toward other offers.

> As usual, online world, offer flexibility, and scientific method apply fully.

More Referrals (tool #6)

> This is again as simple, or as complex, as the follow-up concept and strategy. It's a different follow-up in comparison with re-igniting customers, but the difference is rather in the content, not in the form.

> Our objective is the referrals, and we design the follow-up accordingly.

> As usual, online world, offer flexibility, and scientific method apply fully.

Better Offers (tool #7)

> This is the very concept and strategy of the offer flexibility. Our offers are to become less selfish and more altruistic -

we're taking less and giving more. In its extreme, we're giving value without taking anything in return - purely altruistic.

Of course, we eventually develop relationships and take the clients to our direct offers, yet it's a matter of skillful follow-up strategies.

As usual, online world, offer flexibility, follow-up, and scientific method apply fully.

Better offers give us a MUCH larger audience, and enable us to build quality relationships, resulting in so much easier and greater results.

More Salespeople (tool #8)

As you may have noticed, it's very difficult to hire a great salesperson. It really is. But does it have to be that difficult?

Here is how to make it easier and simpler.

There is no such thing as the best salesperson in absolute terms. There is the best salesperson for you, for your business. As such, your hiring processes, from the beginning to the end, should mirror the experience your future salesperson will have to go through with your prospects. This is exactly how to attract the perfect salespeople for you, and to filter out those who don't fit the bill. This is exactly how and why the new hires will be aligned with your company and your requirements "automatically", and also how to avoid a lot of pain and frustration.

Thus, the ideal hiring process will incorporate a bold promise on the one hand, and resistance, adversity, and even a lack of common sense that your potential hire needs to overcome, on the other hand.

This is why your sales experience itself needs to be understood and clarified before you can map out your hiring process.

At the same time, the ideal sales process may include a few distinct roles, and all the roles may require skills and qualities of a different nature. Some roles may be effectively outsourced, while others may not. For example, one of my favorite sales processes includes a data miner, a data scraper, an appointment setter, a presenter, a closer, a trainer, and, finally, a manager. There are seven distinct roles right here. While the first three roles can be outsourced, the latter four usually can't.

This is not to say that your sales process must have 7+ professionals doing the sales. Sometimes, just one five-star salesperson is all you need. But whatever it is, you need to understand and clarify your own sales process, and design the hiring and training processes accordingly.

Better Salespeople (tool #9)

Here, we're focusing on how to dramatically improve your existing sales force. There are a few aspects to consider.

First of all, the salespeople shouldn't feel like they are in a vacuum. Even the best and the brightest champions should still be members of the team. Regular weekly meetings are a must. These meetings are simple and easy to conduct, yet they yield amazing, exponential improvements. You don't even have to prepare for those meetings. Here is the sample content:

- Reviewing stats.
- Reviewing techniques.
- Reviewing difficulties.
- Sharing funniest episodes.
- Coming up with Aha-moments.
- Collective brainstorming of any unresolved issues, problems, difficulties.
- Designing the procedures, fine-tuning the processes, and discussing suggested corrections and additions.

Regular monthly trainings, workshops, and demonstrations are a must.

There are many very simple and amazingly effective frameworks for conducting trainings and workshops in case you don't want to invest in a 3rd party, which would take care of those for you. Even if you've never conducted anything like that, it will take you just a few minutes to prepare for a successful event of that nature.

Replicating success.

You have to capture, document, and organize everything happening in your business.

Capturing the brain trust behind success has far-reaching implications. Some of the effects are:

- it helps fine-tune and improve the results even further;
- it helps understand what brings success;
- It enables others to follow a similar path;
- It helps develop training materials and train new hires;
- It allows you to stay focused and allocate resources efficiently;
- it helps to understand better what has to be done and how;
- It helps create marketing materials and other relevant content.

It's really simple: anything that works must be captured, understood, documented, organized, fine-tuned, and replicated. This is how the success of one salesperson (who is sometimes a CEO in the case of a startup or in earlier stages of business development) is understood and replicated in others.

However, the subject of replicating success is not limited to your sales team. Everything we've said on the subject can be said about ANY business activity, hence the next section, "leverage & multiply".

Leverage & Multiply (tool #10)

Scripting

> When anything works, and is captured, understood, documented, and organized, it can also be scripted and, often, automated.
>
> Scripting is a subject on its own. It's important to realize that when we talk about scripting, sometimes it means a script that must be followed word for word, without any deviations, and sometimes we mean rather a framework or sequence of steps which is not meant to be a literal word-for-word script.
>
> The style of scripting, and other relevant details, depend on the context, but the main point is that whenever there is any communication, there must be a script! The system of great scripts is essential to create a leverage and multiply your success.

Automation

> Automation is another powerful tool to leverage and multiply success.
>
> If there is success, that is to say, if something works - it can be automated. But even the best automation must be fine-tuned; it may not work as desired right away.
>
> There are two common mistakes that can be observed:
>
> - Mass marketing and sales are not preceded by 1-on-1 developmental approach. (It might still work, but takes much longer and requires a bigger investment.)
> - 1-on-1 marketing and sales are not followed by a mass approach. (Any localized success can always be scaled, leveraged, and even automated.)

When working with automations, the following distinction is important:

At times it makes sense to build a whole automation, and fine-tune it afterwards.

However, at other times it's better to assume a gradual building by extension and expansion.

Here is a simple example. A sales automation is meant to make a sale. However, such an automation may need too many steps, and it's difficult to predict how to structure the whole thing in a way that would work. It may make sense in the first phase to create a solid flow of leads, by building a lead capture automation.

In the next phase, some, or all of the remaining "manual", in-person steps will be gradually automated to reflect the real sales experience, each step considering the live experience and feedback.

It's possible that some steps would never be automated, especially for high-ticket sales, and some would be only partially automated. In certain other cases, the process may be fully automated, fine-tuned, and scaled to a desired degree.

CHAPTER 10

Finances for a CEO

The ultimate goal of accounting

Here is what the numbers in general, and the financial statements in particular, should IDEALLY achieve for your company.

You surely know your business. You surely know what's important.

ANYTHING OF IMPORTANCE should be reflected in your numbers, and you must know where exactly, that is to say, which report, which line, which number, or which ratio.

And if anything of importance is not reflected anywhere - you should create that report, that line, that number, or that ratio.

At the same time, you must know how each number, each line, and each ratio in the financial statements correlates to the reality of your business. No, not in general. You have to know what exactly it corresponds to, and, in addition, what assumptions and estimates it's based on and why. You also have to be clear on where every decision you make ends up in the financial statements.

Of course, not everything will be important. In fact, even important numbers should be combined in certain ways to diminish how many data points you need to analyze the situations and base your decisions on. However, at least in order to decide what's important and what's not, you have to understand and fine-tune it all.

But it goes further. Once the reality of your business is reflected in the financial statements, there are many insights that you can gain from the numbers that when projected back into your business will add important and even crucial variables and aspects that you would never be aware of, if not for the numbers. Your whole perception of what is important and what's not will most probably change dramatically once you freely move between the domain of your business and the domain of your numbers.

You may think that to achieve such a lofty goal you would need to become a financial professional.

No, you would not!

From your perspective, accounting as a profession should give you the framework and practical examples, but the real mastery will come from your insight into the business, combined with the accounting framework, by correlating the business reality and the numbers.

This is how the science and the art of finance becomes a very effective and powerful tool.

The non-factual nature of the financial statements

Even the most basic figure, a company's revenue in any given period, reflects a whole host of estimates and assumptions. So too a company's profit.

Profit is based on revenue. Revenue is recognized when a product or service is delivered, not when the bill is paid. So, the top line of the income statement is often no more than a promise. The revenue figure doesn't reflect real money and neither does the profit at the bottom.

But this is the most "innocent" of observations. Almost all the important numbers - surprise! - are based on assumptions and estimates.

You're expected to make decisions based on the numbers, aren't you? As well as direct your subordinates and plan the future of your department or company. But how are you supposed to do just that, if two financial professionals, "cooking" the company's books, may come up with two totally different sets of reports that present different pictures of reality?

This may go as far as to present a difficulty in identifying the reports as belonging to the very same company. Moreover, this does NOT mean that either of the professionals has done anything incorrectly or falsified the numbers!

This is why EVEN if you have a CFO, a controller, a treasurer, and a host of accountants, you still have to get involved with the numbers. No, you don't have to become a CFO; your CFO and accountants will still do the job, but you have to understand the structure of the information, what it is based on, what assumptions and estimates are in the foundation of the financial system of your company. You may also need to correct some assumptions and estimates, to be able to make better decisions and achieve greater results.

The goal of this exploration is not to teach you the science of finance and the art of accounting, but rather to give you all the main points where and why the numbers become subtle, the points that trigger the necessity for assumptions and estimates to be made.

Understanding these simple concepts will give you control over the numbers and over the picture and implications that emerge from the numbers.

One of the most common issues that cause financial distortions and misconceptions is a mismatch of the costs and the revenues. Hence, one of the main accounting principles, which is simple in concept, yet subtle and difficult to implement right, is the matching principle: the costs should be matched to the associated revenue. This is how the income statement becomes a piece of art.

Revenue recognition

Revenue or sales refers to the value of what a company sold to its customers during a given time period. The sale is recognized when the product or service is delivered.

But what if the delivery happens over time? What if it takes days? Months? Years? For example, providing service over time. Or supplying parts of the order at different times. Or selling a piece of equipment bundled with maintenance. When is such a sale a sale? How much of the price covered the cost of equipment, and how much was for the included subsequent services?

There is no correct answer. It's a judgment call. You have to split up the revenue into chunks, and allocate it to appropriate time periods.

A slight shift in perception of revenue recognition allowed Xerox to make a "mistake" worth $6 billion.

Stop for a moment. Reflect on this:

Without any actual changes in objective reality, just by rewriting the books, a company can "generate" billions of dollars in profit virtually overnight.

Classifying costs: operating expense vs. capital expenditure

Operating expenses are the costs required to keep the business going from day to day. Operating expenses are listed on the income statement and are subtracted from the revenue to determine profit.

A capital expenditure is the purchase of an item that's considered a long-term investment. Capital expenditures show up on the balance sheet; only the depreciation of a piece of capital equipment appears on the income statement.

Reclassifying a cost from an operating expense into a capital expenditure increases the profit immediately, without any actual changes in reality. Accordingly, moving a cost in the other direction "magically" decreases the profit.

So, what is it? Is it an operating expense of a capital expenditure indeed?

Well, often there is no correct answer. It's a judgment call.

Classifying costs: COGS vs. R&D

Product cost goes into cost of goods sold - COGS. If product costs go up, gross profit goes down.

Development costs, however, go into R&D, which is included in the operating expense section of the income statement and doesn't affect gross profit at all.

The distinction is often subtle. Certain costs seem to equally belong to COGS or R&D.

The implications are not subtle though. For example, classifying them under R&D incorrectly may result in low product pricing, and, subsequently in a lack of profit. At the same time, classifying them under COGS incorrectly may result in abandoning the product line because of inability to compete on pricing.

In general, the idea behind COGS is to measure all the costs directly associated with making the product or delivering the service, the materials and the labor. But the borderline between direct and indirect is fuzzy, and is always open to interpretation.

Accruals and allocations

An accrual is the portion of a revenue or expense item that is recorded in a particular time span.

Allocations are apportionments of costs to different departments or activities within a company.

The purpose of accruals and allocations is to match costs to revenues in a given time period as accurately as possible.

Manipulating accruals and allocations may create vastly different pictures of the very same business. Moreover, neither of the variations may be intrinsically correct or incorrect.

Depreciation

Depreciation is the method used to allocate the cost of assets on the income statement. It is based on the same idea as accruals: we want to match as closely as possible the costs of our products and services with what was actually sold. Instead of recording the total expense right away, we attempt to spread the cost of the expenditure over the useful life of the item.

"Useful life"? What's that? Do we really know how long a thing is going to last?

Assets worth $1,000,000 over a five-year lifespan depreciate $200,000 a year. Increasing the life span to 10 years, however, decreases depreciation to $100,000 a year, thus gaining $100,000 in annual profit without actual change to the business.

Non-cash revenue and expenses

How can revenue be anything other than cash?

Deferred revenue is money that has come in but is as yet unearned. So, it can't go into the income statement. Instead, it's recorded as liability on the balance sheet as deferred revenue. It's only when the service or product is delivered (think of airlines and the tickets purchased in advance) that the appropriate amounts are transferred from the balance sheet to the income statement, but at this point they are non-cash by nature, as the cash was already received earlier.

How can an expense be other than cash?

A non-cash expense is one that is charged to a period of time on the income statement but is not actually paid out in cash. This is because the cash was already paid, but the expense wasn't recorded as such, as it has to be allocated over the asset's life, a chunk at a time. Hence, we deal with amortization, which is the same basic idea as depreciation, but applies to intangible assets.

Manipulating the lifespan of tangible and intangible assets, as well as allocating the costs unevenly throughout the lifespan, opens the flexibility of interpreting the reality to a large degree, possibly resulting in distortion through depreciation and amortization, if taken too far.

The income statement: the meaning of the numbers and the decision-making

Let's introduce the basic definitions first, and then we will consider the relative importance of the numbers from different points of view.

Profit is the amount left over after expenses are subtracted from revenue. There are three basic types of profit: gross profit, operating profit, and net profit. Each one is determined by subtracting certain categories of expenses from revenue.

Gross profit is sales minus cost of goods sold or cost of services. It is what's left over after a company has paid the direct costs incurred in making the product or delivering the service. Gross profit can be greatly affected by decisions about when to recognize revenue and by decisions about what to include in COGS.

Operating profit is gross profit minus operating expenses or SG&A (selling, general & administrative), including depreciation and amortization – which is also known as EBIT (pronounced EE-bit; earnings before interest and taxes).

What has not yet been subtracted from revenue is interest and taxes. Why not? Because operating profit is the profit a company earns from the business it is in - from its operations. Taxes don't have anything to do with how well you're running your business. And interest expenses depend on whether the company is financed with debt or equity. But the financial structure of the company has nothing to do with how well it is run from an operational perspective.

That's why operating profit, or EBIT, is a good gauge of how well a company is being managed.

EBITDA (pronounced EE-bit-dah) on the other hand is earnings before interest, taxes, depreciation, and amortization. It may be a better measure of a company's operating efficiency, because it ignores non-cash charges such as amortization and depreciation altogether.

Net profit is the bottom line of the income statement, what's left after ALL costs and expenses are subtracted from revenue. It's operating profit minus interest, taxes, various one-time charges, and any other costs not included in operating expenses.

Consider five different points of view: marketing, sales, operational, financial efficiency, "survival".

From a marketing and sales point of view, a gross revenue (and its changes over time) is the most meaningful number.

From a sales point of view, a gross profit (and its changes over time) is the most meaningful number.

From an operational point of view, an operational profit (and its changes over time) is the most meaningful number, and the operational expenses become of essence.

From a financial efficiency point of view, a net profit (and its changes over time) is the most meaningful number, and the interest and taxes become of essence.

From a survival point of view, all the previous numbers are almost irrelevant, as even with billions of dollars in profits a company can suffocate and go bankrupt by running out of cash.

If you want to increase profit, you have a choice:

1. Increasing profitable sales.

2. Reducing COGS.

3. Cutting operating expenses, which almost always means reducing the headcount.

What's the easiest of the three?

Obviously, the third one. A CEO taking over troubled companies starts by cutting the payroll in the overhead expense areas. It makes earnings look better fast.

However, it's the most questionable of the three (unless your overhead is genuinely overblown). It will certainly improve the numbers short-term, but it will also certainly hurt your business long-term.

Beware of intangibles

What a company owns is called its assets.

What it owes is called its liabilities.

What it's worth is called owners' equity or shareholders' equity.

The balance sheet is a statement of what a business owns and what it owes at a particular point in time. The difference between what a company owns and what it owes represents equity.

Over time, the equity section of the balance sheet shows the accumulation of profits or losses left in the business; the line is called retained earnings or sometimes accumulated earnings.

Equity is always assets minus liabilities; it is also the sum of all capital paid in by shareholders **plus** any profits earned by the company since its inception **minus** dividends paid out to shareholders.

Current assets include anything that can be turned into cash in less than a year. Long-term assets include physical assets that have a useful life of more than a year - usually anything that is either depreciated or amortized.

Do you feel a bit fuzzy about a distinction between "less than a year" and "more than a year"?

You should. The distinction is not always apparent in practice and is open to interpretation.

A company's intangible assets include anything that has value but that you can't touch or spend: employees' skills, customer lists, proprietary knowledge, patents, brand names, reputation, strategic strengths, and so on. Most of these assets are not found on the balance sheet unless an acquiring company pays for them and records them as goodwill.

Since intangible assets can't be touched, and, generally, can't be sold either, the corresponding numbers become a matter of art, not a matter of science. Take them as such. Understand them well in order to make better decisions based on those numbers.

Ratios

Numbers by themselves don't present the full story. The ratios do.

Watching the numbers and the ratios enables us to perform magic: we can measure economic impact of small changes, which is the backbone of an iterative process which allows us to optimize and fine-tune our business to its optimal performance and perfection. Small improvements can result in millions of dollars in cash or profit, yet this impact is often invisible if you don't watch the numbers carefully.

Profitability ratios demonstrate a company's ability to generate profit, or, in other words, to generate sales and control expenses.

- Gross profit margin is gross profit divided by sales.

- Operating profit margin is operating profit divided by sales.

- Net profit margin is net profit divided by sales.

These three margins are of extreme importance. Each of them reflects a certain aspect of the business.

However, as with any other "standard" numbers, these are just examples. You may want to correlate any meaningful part of the profit (in the context of your business) to any meaningful part of the revenue.

Let's now look at the balance sheet, in combination with the income statement. There are a few great examples that demonstrate how efficiently and effectively your assets are used to generate revenue and profit (in a sense, just like profit margins show how expenses are used to generate revenue and profit).

- Return on assets: the percentage of profit a company earns in relation to its overall resources. It is commonly defined as net income divided by total assets.

- Return on equity: the amount of net income returned as a percentage of shareholders' equity. Return on equity measures a company's profitability by revealing how much profit a company generates with the money shareholders have invested.

- Return on debt: the amount of profit generated for every dollar held by a company in debt.

- Return on capital: indicates how effective a company is at turning capital into profits, as calculated by the formula (Net income - Dividends) / (Debt + Equity).

Some examples may be basic to you, while others may be confusing, but please remember that these are just examples. The numbers and ratios important in your business should be coming from the reality of your business, and not so much from accounting textbooks (though of course there are some universal numbers and ratios that are important for almost any business; also, companies in one industry have a lot in common, so you can always learn from competitors what they deem important).

Debt allows a company to grow beyond what its invested capital alone would allow. The business term for debt is leverage. This is because by using (or leveraging on) the debt, a company can build a large number of assets, thus using a modest amount of capital to build a larger business than would be otherwise possible.

- Financial leverage: the extent to which the company is financed by debt. The most well-known financial leverage ratio is the debt-to-equity ratio, as calculated by the formula (Total debt / Shareholders Equity).
  - o Leverage increases a company's ability to make money, yet increases risks too. You always want some leverage - to amplify your results, but not too much - to minimize your risks.
- Operating leverage: a ratio between fixed costs and variable costs (fixed costs: costs that are constant whatever the quantity of goods or services produced; variable costs: costs that vary with the level of output).
  - o Fixed costs are hard to cut. Variable costs are much easier to cut, if necessary.

- o Consider airlines: high operating leverage and high financial leverage. Airlines commonly use what's called an operating lease: instead of buying an airplane they lease it from an investor. Why? Just to keep the ratios in place! Well, you may ask that doesn't change the reality much, does it? You're right, that's why it's very important to correlate the numbers and the reality with confidence and ease!
- Interest coverage: how much interest a company has to pay every year, relative to how much it's making, as calculated by the formula (Operating profit / annual interest charges). This indicates how easy it is for a company to pay off the interest.

Some ratios indicate liquidity. Can a company pay its bills? Is a company running out of cash?

- Current ratio: current assets / current liabilities (Current assets can be converted into cash within a year; current liabilities must be paid back within a year.)
  - o If less than 1, red flag: the company is running out of cash within a year.
  - o If too high, you should ask the question: why is the company sitting on cash instead of giving it to investors or investing it in the business?
- Quick ratio: a company's ability to meet its short-term obligations with its most liquid assets. Because we're only concerned with the most liquid assets, the ratio excludes inventory, as calculated by the formula ((current assets - inventory) / liabilities).

Some ratios indicate efficiency. How efficiently you manage certain assets and liabilities?

- Days Inventory Outstanding: an efficiency ratio that measures the average number of days the company holds its inventory before selling it. The ratio measures the number of days funds are tied up in inventory, as calculated by the formula (average inventory / COGS / days). Just like many other numbers and ratios, calculating and focusing on this one may bring unexpected, if not shocking results. A minute change to Days Inventory Outstanding can dramatically increase the working capital and solve cash flow issues, if any.

- Days payable outstanding: a company's average payable period that measures how long it takes a company to pay its invoices from suppliers and other creditors, as calculated by the formula (Ending Accounts Payable / COGS / days). This is a very interesting indicator to optimize. You may think that the higher the number of days payable, the better, but it's not that simple. Cash-wise, it's definitely better. Your cash position will skyrocket. But keeping suppliers happy may be a rewarding objective in its own right; in fact, making suppliers unhappy may be damaging to the business, which is not worth sacrificing to earn a higher cash position. The balance is far from obvious.

- Inventory turnover: a ratio showing how many times a company's inventory is sold and replaced over a period of time, usually over a year. The days in the period can then be divided by the inventory turnover formula to calculate the days it takes to sell the inventory on hand. It is calculated as sales divided by average inventory. Interesting that the last inventory turnover reported by Walmart was 8.19, Target - 5.62, Amazon - 8.66.

To reiterate, all the numbers and ratios we've considered, and multitudes of others, which have remained behind the curtain, are just examples. Your job is to develop a system of data points, numbers and ratios, that correspond to your business, helping you create a digital dashboard of your business, which will project back to the reality of your business and give you new insights, more understanding, robust decision-making criteria, and a great management tool.

Before we wrap up the section on finances, here is one more concept of paramount importance which must be understood deeply. It's the centerpiece of entrepreneurship, and it's the heart of running a successful company.

ROI - Return on investment

Return on investment, as a concept, determines a frame of mind, which dictates necessity to develop an approach and a process of deciding what capital investments to make in order to improve the value of the company.

The foundation of capital budgeting contains the capital budgeting tools, as well as capital budgeting decision methods.

Each tool by itself, as well as each method by itself, is simple. Yet, the framework built around the tools and the methods is very powerful and profound.

- Capital budgeting tools
  - Time value of money
    - The time value of money is the idea that money available at the present time is worth more than the same amount in the future, due to its potential earning capacity. In other words, provided money can earn interest, any amount of money is worth more the sooner it's received. In other words, when it comes to money, the sooner the better.
    - If PV is present value, FV is future value, and r is interest rate for a certain time period between present and future, then, by definition, $FV = PV * (1+r)$.
    - The same formula, applied to n time periods, looks as follows: $FV = PV * (1+r)^n$. Basic algebra, based on this formula, allows us to make three types of calculations:
      1. Calculate future value, given present value, a rate, and time. This shows the future value of cash we have on hand. In this sense, the FV in the future equals PV in the present. This is the present value projected into the future.
      2. Calculate present value, given future value and a rate. This shows how much we have to invest in order to have a specified output at a given time, with a given rate. In this sense,

the FV in the future equals PV in the
present. This is the future value
projected into the present.

3. Calculate a required rate of return
which enables us to invest a specified
amount and receive a specified output
in a given time.

- The concept of time value of money is crucial
for the Return on Investment mindset and the
framework. It's precisely this concept and the
three types of calculations that need to be
applied when we say "bring the value / cash
flow to the present", "bring the value / cash
flow to the future", etc. For example, $1,000
now "equals" $1,100" in a year from now
with 10% interest rate (simply 10% annual
increase). For the very same reason, $1,100 in
a year from now "equals" $1,000 now with
10% rate. This is how we take the value and
bring it forward and backward in time. The
same $1,100 in a year from now "equals"
$1,210 in two years from now - simply a 10%
increase from $1,100 (1,100 * 1.1 = 1,210).

- When we deal with more complex cash flows,
solving the resulting equations may present a
challenge to you. However, I don't want to
dedicate another chapter to developing the
algebra skills, as you don't have to do it
yourself anyway. As long as you understand
the essence, you're in control. You can always
find somebody who will take care of
technicalities for you.

o Hurdle rate

- Hurdle rate is the minimum rate that a
company expects to earn when investing in an
opportunity. The hurdle rate is also referred
to as the company's required rate of return, or
a target rate. In order for a project to be

accepted, its internal rate of return must equal or exceed the hurdle rate.

- An alternative term in use is "minimum acceptable rate of return", abbreviated MARR.
- The hurdle rate is usually determined by evaluating existing opportunities, rate of return for investments, and other relevant factors.
- Higher risks are associated with a higher hurdle rate. Lower risks are associated with a lower hurdle rate. As a benchmark, a traditional inflation-free rate of interest for risk-free loans may be considered at 3-5%.

o Opportunity cost
   - Opportunity cost is an unrealized value associated with the choice of a best alternative cost. It is the "cost" incurred by not enjoying the benefit that would have been realized by taking the next best available choice, or the loss of potential gain from other alternatives when one specific alternative is chosen.

o Cost of equity
   - The cost of equity is a rate of return a company theoretically pays to its equity investors, to compensate for the risk they undertake by investing their capital.

o Cost of debt
   - When companies borrow funds from outside lenders, the interest rate paid on these funds is called the cost of debt. Since debt expense is usually tax-deductible, the cost of debt is computed on an after-tax basis, to make it comparable with the cost of equity. Thus, debt is discounted by the appropriate tax rate.

o Cost of capital
   - If capital is composed of 100% debt, the cost of capital is the cost of debt. If capital is composed of 100% equity, the cost of capital

is the cost of equity. However, if capital is composed of a combination of equity and debt, we need to calculate weighted average cost of capital, which takes into consideration how much of the capital is equity, and how much of the capital is debt.

- If debt is D, cost of debt is K_d, equity is E, cost of equity is K_e, and tax rate is T, weighted average cost of capital is calculated as WACC $= D*K_D*(1-T)/(D+E) + E*K_e/(D+E)$. If this is the first time you're seeing this formula, just give it a couple of minutes to sink in. It's very logical and intuitively clear after you give it some time to reflect on it.
- The WACC is the rate that a company is expected to pay on average to its security holders to finance its assets. That's why it's often called the firm's cost of capital.
- The WACC represents the minimum return that a company must earn to satisfy its creditors, owners, and other providers of capital, OR THEY WILL INVEST ELSEWHERE.
- As apparent from the formula, the WACC is calculated taking into account the relative weights of each component of the capital structure.
- Companies can (and should) use WACC to see if the projects available to them are worthwhile to undertake.

- Capital budgeting decision methods
  - Payback period (PB)
    - Payback period refers to the period of time required to reach the break-even point, i.e. to recoup the funds expended in an investment. This is the simplest and the least useful budgeting method, though it is always a good starting point.
  - Net present value (NPV)

- Once the concept "Time value of money" is understood well, along with its formula and the way to calculate present value, given future value and a rate, the NPV method is almost obvious. A series of cash flow events should be brought back to present and added up.
- For example, $100,000 invested brings $20,000 after the 1st year, $30,000 after the 2nd year, and $70,000 after the 3rd year.
    1. The NPV is calculated as follows (based on 10% rate): $20,000 after the 1st year equals $20,000/1.1^1 = $18,181.82 now; $30,000 after the 2nd year equals $30,000/1.1^2 = $24,793.39 now; $70,000 after 3rd year equals $70,000/1.1^3 = $52,592.04 now. The whole cash flow brought into "now" is summed up: -$100,000 + $18,181.82 + $24,793.39 + $52,592.04 = -$4,432.75, which is a negative value.
    2. When NPV is positive, the project is justified. When NPV is negative, the project is not justified. Why? Because investing the same $100,000 at the hurdle rate brings up better return than our proposed project's cash flow.
    3. Just to spell it out, let's say we're investing $100,000 at 10% hurdle rate. We get $110,000 after the 1st year. Let's subtract $20,000 (corresponding to the proposed project's cash flow). Remaining $90,000 will give us $99,000 after the 2nd year. Let us subtract $30,000 (corresponding to the proposed project's cash flow). Remaining $69,000 will give us $75,900 - against the 3rd payment of $70,000 in our proposed project's cash

flow. So, we're easily getting $5,900 more elsewhere; why should we bother with the project?

4. Note that NPV came out negative $4,432.75. This was the difference expressed in "now" moment. If we take this amount, $4,432.75 and invest it at 10% rate for 3 years, we're getting exactly $5,900 at the end. So this is exactly the same value expressed in different time points - in the present, and in the future.

5. It's interesting that this resolution is counter-intuitive. The loss of opportunity is not visible to an eye. The cash flow looks healthy. In fact, it looks like we're making a lot of money after three years.

6. The bottom line: stay away from such a project. But first, make sure that your hurdle rate is 10% indeed. Figuring out the hurdle rate is a subject on its own…

○ Internal rate of return (IRR)

   ▪ Once the concept "Time value of money" is understood well, along with its formula and the way to calculate a required rate of return which enables us to invest a specified amount and receive a specified output in a given time, the IRR method is almost obvious. The IRR is an interest rate that sets Net Present Return to zero. In other words, we're looking for an interest rate which produces the very same cash flow as our proposed project, no less and no more.

   ▪ In our example (-$100,000 + $20,000 + $30,000 + $70,000) the equation which allows us to calculate the IRR is as follows:

1. $20,000/(1+r)^1 + 30,000/(1+r)^2 + 70,000/(1+r)^3 = 100,000$

2. The logic of the equation is straightforward: we bring the cash flow from future to present, assuming that the interest rate is unknown, while supposing that the present value of the whole cash flow in the present equals the investment required in our proposed project. This allows us to find the unknown interest rate.

3. By solving this equation, we find that the IRR equals 7.5%. This means that our proposed project generates the cash flow based on a 7.5% interest rate. In our example, since the hurdle rate is 10%, the project is not worth it. An alternative investment at the 10% hurdle rate will produce better results.

- o Modified Internal rate of return (MIRR)
  - It's the same idea as IRR, but with a twist.
  - In IRR we take all the cash flow and bring it back to the present, while finding the interest rate which would allow the present value of the cash flow to match the proposed investment.
  - In MIRR we take the cash flow and bring it forward to the future, i.e. allowing the cash flow to compound until the end of the last time period the project covers. Then we look for the interest rate which would achieve the same very result from the investment which is equal to the investment of the proposed project. This rate is MIRR.
  - In our example, assuming that the reinvestment rate is the same, 10% (in real life the reinvestment rate will probably be different from the rate of the initial financing - perhaps WACC), $20,000 after the 1st year

equals $24,200 after the 3rd year; $30,000 after the 2nd year equals $33,000 after the 3rd year, so the final value of the whole cash flow is $24,200 + $33,000 + $70,000 = $127,200, and the equation to find MIRR is $100,000*(1+r)^3 = $127,200$, which sets MIRR to 8.35%.

- This is still lower than 10%, so in our example the project is not worth it according to MIRR too, yet note that 8.35% is higher than IRR, which was 7.5%. This is due to the fact that we allow cash flow to compound, which is not the case with the IRR method.

This concludes the subject of ROI - return on investment. It's a bit technical, and may take some skill to solve some equations, yet it's important to understand the essence of the matter. We're simply comparing a proposed project with alternative opportunities. We want to make sure that whatever we do, it's the best among the available options. An alternative opportunity is generally represented by an investment with a given rate of return, which corresponds to our hurdle rate. The rest is technicalities.

CHAPTER 11

Value Revolution

T his chapter is based on the work of Neil Rackham and John De Vincentis.

The business reality is changing right in front of our eyes, yet the nature and the extent of the changes are not commonly understood.

In this day and age, customers are changing. These changes are deep and fundamental. They affect every level of purchasing, from the individual customer to the giant corporation.

The common denominator throughout these changes is AWARENESS OF VALUE. The increasing sophistication of customers in their search for value poses significant threats to companies trying to use traditional selling strategies to compete in the new value-driven marketplace.

Decades ago, information was scarce. Getting fully informed in any product category was difficult, if not impossible. People used their instincts, relied on brand name, sought the advice of friends and relatives, and the last, but not the least, appreciated getting the information they needed from salespeople and sales promotional materials.

Today, those good old days are gone. Available information is limitless. Customers are informed, even over-informed. With the information sources that today's consumers are using, the traditional approaches of manufacturers together with the messages their salespeople deliver appears redundant and futile.

That's why traditional sales approaches are more and more ineffective. A sales force can no longer survive solely to communicate product value when customers already have, or can quickly and easily get all the information they need to make a confident decision.

This new information age is forcing a reassessment of the traditional thinking about sales and its role in providing customers with such information.

Sales vs. the rest of the organization

The 20th-century purpose of a sales force was to communicate the value of your offerings. Selling has been about value communication.

This takes sales apart from the rest of the organization. Because other functions in the organization, such as manufacturing, engineering, product development, or even human resources, have been restructuring and realigning themselves to create more value for customers, activities that don't add value have been reduced or eliminated. Hence, the whole organization is about CREATING VALUE, while the sales is about COMMUNICATING VALUE.

Companies that don't realize that the reality has been changing become more and more frustrated with their marketing and sales. Just communicating value inherent in their products and services isn't enough anymore. Increasingly, companies are coming to realize that their survival depends on their capacity to create customer value in every part of their enterprise, INCLUDING THEIR SALES.

Selling is in the early stages of complete transformation. The very meaning and purpose of selling is shifting. Customers are increasingly no longer interested in entering the sales process, if the sales process does not possess its distinct value for them. **The value migrates from the product itself to how the product is acquired.**

The bottom line is, the sales process is no longer about communicating value - it's about creating value, just like for the rest of the organization.

From the great idea to the formula

The idea that the sales force must create value, not just communicate it, makes perfect sense until... Until you try to figure out what you should actually do with it.

Here is the simple formula, the definition of value:

$$VALUE = BENEFITS - COST.$$

Cost in this formula is not only about money. It's a combination of time, money, and effort of any kind - just whatever the customer has to lose to realize the benefits.

Obviously, there are two ways to increase value:

1. More benefits

2. Less cost

Which of the two ways would you choose?

This is not a trivial question. In fact, this distinction is fundamental and translates into success or failure in modern marketing and sales.

Whether it's better to create new benefits or provide cheaper and easier acquisition depends entirely on the customer.

Why?

Simply because the value creation model must match the customer's value expectations. And if not - there is no sale.

Corresponding to this crucial distinction, there are two types of customers:

1. Intrinsic value customers:
   o They already understand the product and how it fits their needs. They are not interested in advice or customization. The greatest value for them is low selling cost and easy acquisition.
2. Extrinsic value customers:

- o They look for value beyond the product or service itself. They need advice and customization. The most effective selling strategy will be one where the sales force is trained, equipped, and compensated to create new value.

There are two types of selling, corresponding to these two types of customers:

1. Transactional selling.
   - o The issues in transactional selling are about cost reduction - how to strip cost out of the sales process and to make the transaction risk and hassle-free for the customer.
2. Consultative selling.
   - o Salespeople have an intimate grasp of the customer's business situation. A mutual investment of time and effort by both seller and customer implies. Listening and gaining understanding are more important selling skills than persuasion; creativity is more important than product knowledge. There are three primary ways to create additional value:
     - i. To help customers understand their problems, issues, and opportunities in a new way.
     - ii. To help customers arrive at new or better solutions to their problems than they would have discovered on their own.
       - Basically, the sales force can help customers to understand the problem domain better, to understand the solutions domain better, and to bridge the problems and the solutions in their particular situation. These are three distinct elements and can be actually implemented on different levels.
     - iii. To act as customers' advocate inside the supplier organization, ensuring the timely allocation of resources to deliver customized

or unique solutions that meet the customers' special needs.

The dual nature of selling has been crystallized:
- Transactional selling reduces resources allocated to selling because customers don't value the sales effort.
  - Transactional selling creates its value by stripping cost and making acquisition easy.
- Consultative selling adds resources to the selling effort, matching the customer's willingness to invest time and effort in the acquisition process.
  - Consultative selling creates new value through the ability of the sales force to advise, customize, and bring expertise beyond the product. The customer, in turn, invests time in educating the supplier during the sales process. So, both parties put more resources into the buying and selling effort.

Two recipes for a disaster

Recipe for a disaster #1.

It's fatal to adopt one value-selling mode if your customers want another:

- A sales force can't fundamentally transform customers who have decided to purchase transactionally into ones who purchase consultatively.

- A sales force can't fundamentally transform customers who have decided to purchase consultatively into ones who purchase transactionally.

Customers buying transactionally may view salespeople as an unnecessary cost and will often perceive sales efforts as value drains. These customers will perceive value only in those salespeople who can make acquisition as cheap, efficient, and trouble-free as possible. They'll often be more comfortable to buy without a salesperson altogether, if possible.

In contrast, the extrinsic value customer wants advice, help, and problem-solving capability from salespeople. Such a customer will see a salesperson as a valuable resource, perhaps more valuable than the products itself.

The key to success is to figure out which selling approach best fits the customer and then create the most value, matching the customer's value expectations.

Recipe for a disaster #2.

The selling strategies can't be simply imagined. The selling strategies must match the buying strategies. The starting point should always be a valid model of the buying process, whether it is broad and universal, or more focused and industry-specific.

For example, here is the general buying model, simple and powerful, introduced by Neil Rackham:

1. Recognition of needs.

2. Evaluation of options.

3. Resolution of concerns.

4. Purchase.

5. Implementation / usage.

Failure to start with a buying model will most probably lead to futile efforts.

Value engineering

Obviously, customers always wanted value. But if before they were satisfied with "simple values", now they've become "connoisseurs". A variety of distinctions in the customer's value recognition capability is staggering. The value your customers want, consciously or unconsciously, is multi-dimensional, and exists in spectrums and degrees. This is equally true for B2C and B2B markets. The business world has never seen anything like this until recently. To be successful, you really need to brainstorm, to rethink, to redesign, to re-engineer the value you provide to your customers throughout the entire process.

How to achieve it?

The organization must transfer investment and effort into areas that create value the customers want. At the same time, they must work ruthlessly to contain their cost in areas that their customers don't value.

For transactional sales, effective use of technology can automate tasks and reduce cost and people requirements. The mantra is, "creating customer value by lowering cost and by facilitating acquisition". Moving to lower-cost channels and even eliminating the sales function entirely are not uncommon, as well as drastically reducing the cost of the current sales force.

For consultative sales, the unique value-creating contribution of the sales force lies in their capacity to link solutions and supplier resources to the specific needs they have uncovered.

Consultative selling works best when:

- The product or service can be differentiated from competing alternatives.

- The product or service can be adapted or customized to the needs of the customer.

- The customer is not completely clear about how the product or service provides solutions or adds value.

- The delivery, installation, or use of the product or service requires coordinated support from the selling organization.

- The product or service has benefits that justify the relatively high cost of consultative selling.

To create value, you must first invest in understanding the customer, and that takes time and effort - much more time and effort than most managers realize. Understanding the customer to a point where it's possible to create value may take months and cost tens of thousands of dollars.

The skills

The skills involved in value creation are very different from those used merely to communicate value. You can communicate the value by simply telling. Polished, persuasive, or enthusiastic telling is all that's needed.

In contrast, successful consultative salespeople sell through understanding and insight, not through telling. Practically speaking, they achieve understanding through asking the right questions.

About implementation

A major issue for consultative selling is how to build more value within the institution, so that ordinary mortals can perform well in consultative sales.

There are three principal ways to create value on an institutional level:

1. Coaching and training.

2. Support tools and information.

3. Sales process: to provide salespeople with a customer-centered roadmap - the steps and tasks for effective consultative selling.

The traditional processes need to be redefined and redesigned in terms of customer value. Prospecting and cold calling is replaced with Value Identification Process, allowing salespeople to identify potential areas of value creation.

It's crucial to understand that a well-designed sales process allows ordinary mortals to do work that is otherwise the sole preserve of the rock stars. A well-articulated process not only guides salespeople; it also gives a framework for their training, coaching, and development.

What's a big deal?

To summarize,
- The sales process must provide value to customers (vs. merely communicating value);
- There are two types of value in the context:
  - More benefits (advice, customization, deepening understanding of the problem domain, deepening understanding of the solution domain, explaining the causes and implications, helping to bridge the problem and the solution, etc.)
    - Customers who want this, we call extrinsic customers, and the process is called consultative selling.
  - Less cost (literally less money, as well as less time and less effort required, ease and convenience of an acquisition, simplicity and speed of the transaction, ease of use, etc.)
    - Customers who want this, we call intrinsic customers, and the process is called transactional selling.

You may ask, why is this a big deal? Isn't this simple and even obvious, that some customers want more help, and some customers want less help?

Yes, this is obvious. Yet, it's easy to overlook the following:

The distinction itself is simple, just like many other life-changing distinctions. However, its simplicity is misleading, because the implications of understanding this distinction fully and applying it to your business explicitly and skillfully are profound. And even if the concept is simple, its application is far from being quick or easy.

The meaning of this distinction is deep and far-reaching. Its advancement is indicating the beginning of the next stage in the history of capitalism. Customers not only dictate WHAT value should be created, but also HOW this value should be communicated and delivered, in all the shades and flavors. Customers demand the HOW to contain the value on its own, and, to make it more complicated, they perceive quite a few distinctions in the value itself.

The deeper meaning of this phenomenon is that the power is shifting even further from manufacturers, suppliers, and service providers to the consumers.

Appendix

The CEO's Guide to The World of Ideas, or... Ideas Are Cheap

There is a general consensus among people of achievement about the superiority of implementation over ideas.

Jeff Bezos: "It's easy to have ideas. It's very hard to turn an idea into a successful product."

Larry Ellison: "Translating a good idea into a great product is unbelievably hard."

Guy Kawasaki, in response to somebody with presumably a great idea: "I hate to tell you, but you have very little. Ideas are easy. Implementation is hard."

These high-achieving people are right, but let me challenge your understanding of what they really mean.

Their message is that an idea exists in the world of potential and, in reality, it's very difficult to actualize it, to bring it down to earth. That's why simply having a great idea does not automatically equal success. In fact, having a great idea is very far from success. There usually are myriads of obstacles and reasons why it might fail, regardless of the quality of the idea per se.

At the same time, having a great idea is necessary for a great success. While having an idea doesn't necessarily guarantee success, not having an idea does guarantee failure in some way, earlier or later.

Furthermore, coming up with a great idea is unbelievably hard. It only seems easy after the fact, because great ideas are usually very simple.

The idea, its quality, and its alignment are shaping your business subtly and powerfully. It may well be beyond your conscious awareness, yet the idea defines everything in your business and around it, as well as everything you go through.

Let's consider some great ideas that people of achievement brought into the world and appreciate their beauty and power.

Brian Chesky (Airbnb)

What's the idea behind Airbnb?

This is how the founder's mother perceived the idea when Brian Chesky shared with her what he was up to: "...So you built this website so that strangers can sleep in your home because you don't have enough money for rent..."

Luckily, Brian saw the idea differently. Let's take a closer look.

Brian's initial idea was, "What if you can book somebody's home just like you can book a hotel room?"

The idea was obvious under the circumstances, as all the hotels in the area were fully booked and arriving people had nowhere to stay.

This was the idea that he implemented with his own apartment, ending up renting it to a few strangers. However, he was very perceptive, and fine-tuned the idea immediately after the experience. The difference was subtle yet profound. The new idea was best expressed by Ashton Kutcher, in his conversation with Brian Chesky: "Bringing people together by opening our homes and hearts to one another".

This may sound idealistic, and perhaps even far-fetched to some people, yet THIS was the idea that was worth billions and changed the hospitality industry forever. Had Brian remained with his original idea of booking a home like a hotel, he wouldn't have gone very far.

Why?

For two reasons. First, the original idea was very weak and wouldn't survive the competition with the hotel chains. Second, Brian Chesky would never have been able to go through everything he had to go through before success came to him and his amazing startup.

Analyzing the profound experience he had with sharing his own home, he was perceptive enough to come up with the new idea which was aligned with the experience he had. Furthermore, he did realize early enough that he was not in the hotel industry, that he didn't compete with hotels at all.

Who did he compete with?

Well, in a sense, with friends and family where you would most probably stay when you visit their city. The only problem is, how many countries, cities, and communities can you visit if you only stay at homes of your old friends and you are not extroverted enough to make new friends quickly and easily anywhere and anytime?

Airbnb gives you a chance to discover new friends - anywhere, anytime. Friends who will share their homes with you, providing you with the best experience – something that very few of your old friends may be capable of doing.

Interestingly, Brian Chesky is trying to evolve his idea even further. As of this writing, its final edition is not yet fully ready. It's still a vague vision. However, it's already fascinating, when you imagine how it can play out in our not-too-far-off-future. The way he sees it, it's about a totally different lifestyle. About people traveling freely around the world without the slightest need to actually own a permanent home. This is when owning a home no longer offers any advantages, in comparison with finding a home to stay or to live, short term or long term. Owning a home becomes unnecessary, just like owning a car in some areas makes no sense any more – in those areas covered by Airbnb's cousin, Uber.

Just imagine smooth, comfortable, convenient, friendly, cheap home sharing with just the level of privacy you require.

The transformation is still on the way, but it's becoming more and more tangible. We'll see what the future brings...

Larry Ellison (Oracle)

The idea of relational databases wasn't new. In fact, Larry Ellison found it in its entirety in the works of Edgar F. Codd who developed the revolutionary approach to data arrangement while working for IBM.

IBM didn't ignore the work of Edgar F. Codd either. There were a few papers published, it was presented on conferences, and there was even the team at IBM that was implementing the new approach to data.

So, what's the difference? Why was IBM so slow, clearly unable to recognize the upcoming revolution, the treasure that was born and developed in their midst?

To be sure, if IBM saw what Larry Ellison saw, Larry wouldn't have had a chance. But they didn't. The difference was in the ideas. IBM perceived one idea, while Larry Ellison perceived another idea.

Let's understand IBM's position. Their key idea was HARDWARE. Or, more precisely, HARDWARE SUPREMACY. The world was divided into hardware and non-hardware - there was nothing else. Of course, good software was always needed; after all, hardware without software is dead, but... Software was secondary. It didn't have the value on its own. Hardware reigned supreme!

Let's sidetrack for a moment, by considering Microsoft before we go back to Oracle.

This is exactly where Microsoft entered the stage, as Bill Gates saw things differently. Bill Gates introduced a funny idea, one that nobody ever had before him. The idea was: software reigns supreme; hardware is secondary; software is a thing on its own!

As a side note, it's not about who is right and who is wrong. It's about WHEN. Because during the earlier stages, hardware was everything indeed, and this was where IBM excelled - IBM's contribution to the world was no less than revolutionary. However, the times changed. If IBM had perceived the change, Bill Gates wouldn't have a chance. But IBM didn't.

Moreover, IBM made what seemed to be mistakes in dealings with Microsoft, by entering into the contracts that put IBM at a disadvantage, and even fueled Microsoft's meteoric rise.

Those weren't mistakes though. IBM was consistent with their IDEA, while Bill Gates was pursuing his own IDEA. They saw the same very phenomena, yet they had two totally different ideas, and those ideas subtly but powerfully shaped their companies, all their dealings and business activities, and the future of the industry, and the future of the world, for that matter.

This was very similar to what happened between IBM and Oracle later on. The RDBMS approach was to the world of data arrangement what the software in general and operating system in particular was to the world of raw hardware. It was a thing on its own. And it was of primary importance now. In fact, this was a revolution. Because a relational database, with its schema and logical organization, disconnected from physical information storage, introduces the standardized layer on which data applications can now be based.

More specifically, when you needed to develop a data application before the RDBMS revolution, you would have to start from scratch, to a large extent, while now you have the whole logical data layer that does the magic for you flexibly and powerfully. Developing data applications becomes a breeze, in comparison to massive, heavily customized effort that needed to be extended in the pre-relational-database world.

IBM was loyal to their credo, to their founding idea, in fact, to the idea that took them to greatness. Yet, this rich and powerful company was powerless and virtually non-competitive when facing somebody with a different idea in mind, the idea that created a different vision of the world - but only for the mind that possessed it.

Of course, "translating a good idea into a great product is unbelievably hard", as Larry Ellison said much later. And we should definitely believe him, as he knew what it took. His contribution to the world has been immense.

Yet, IBM was an 800-pound gorilla, and no matter how hard Larry was ready to work, IBM was capable of working much harder. But it didn't help. Larry won.

He still had to work hard to take the idea to fruition, but his victory was firmly rooted in the world of ideas. The lesson is of paramount importance: once you win in the world of ideas, only then can you, and should, work hard.

Marc Benioff (Salesforce), Bill McDermott (SAP), Alan Trefler (Pegasystems)

Let's compare the definitive ideas behind the three remarkable companies.

Salesforce has been almost a synonym for CRM - customer relationship management. In the Salesforce universe, a customer is everything. The universe is viewed as customers' journeys. A customer journey is mapped out, designed, redesigned, and treasured. Let's call the key idea "customer's journey".

SAP's idea is "running the world better", or, as fine-tuned by Bill McDermott, "helping the world to run better". This may be their mission, yet the idea expressed this way lacks substance. When we dig deeper, a more substantial idea is showing up:

A business is viewed as a system of interconnected processes which are to be reflected digitally. In other words, the idea is in creating a perfect digital reflection of the reality, that is to say, of all the company's processes and activities.

This may seem too intangible, but consider an epitome of the idea - a digital dashboard which shows you EVERYTHING that happens in your business anytime and anywhere - in real time. Let's call the key idea "complete digital reflection". Anything and everything is digitized to the extent that human input is unnecessary beyond actual core activities that human beings are actually performing. All is immediately and automatically digitally captured, digitally managed, and digitally directed.

But don't forget, on a higher level, SAP is not even about running the company - it's about running the world! This is where the focus on interaction and collaboration between the companies comes into play, to achieve total automation and digitization of not only what's happening in the companies, but also what's happening between the companies.

Pegasystems is introducing the idea of a model. Any particular business has its own model, which is an abstraction that describes all the business activities. The brilliance of Pegasystems is in separating business model and technology. You, as a business, don't have to deal with technology at all. You deal with an abstract layer - with a logical business model. The magic happens behind the curtain: all the technology is taken care of automatically, by auto-translating the abstract model into the language of technology. This way, technological innovations, disruptions, revolutions, all the channels are incorporated and aligned automatically, without you having to change anything. All you, a business, have to deal with, is the model which masterfully models your business logic, uniquely designed and built for your business. Let's call the key idea "model".

Briefly, here are the three distinct ideas:

- Salesforce: "customer journey"

- SAP: "complete digital reflection"

- Pegasystems: "model"

Needless to say, all the three companies have great databases, design and map out their customers' journeys, employ digital reflection of business activities, as well as use an advanced model for any given business, effectively minimizing their customers' direct exposure to the raw technologies. In other words, a very close look would suggest to us that all the three companies are doing the same very things.

Yet, in spite of the similarities, their differences are immense, even if subtle. The differences are powerfully rooted in their respective core ideas. I would go as far as to say that these tough competitors don't even compete, or - more precisely - don't have to compete. They have to simply, very clearly, and in a creative manner, communicate a laser focus on their respective ideas to their actual and potential customers. This way, each company will have its share of the market, and even though one of the three will have the biggest share, and one of the three will have the lowest share, the order doesn't translate into an "I-am-better-than-you" framework. All three can be successful and profitable, perfectly serving THEIR respective clients.

So how do you see what your business actually needs? Which of the three would you pick? Would you focus on your customer's journey? Would you like to create a complete digital reflection of your business activities and have a unified dashboard that shows you the entirety of your business in real time? Or would you like to manage a technology-free model of your business, dealing with your business logic and let the system take care of all the technology for you on auto-pilot? What's better for your business?

The answer is, I don't know what's better, because we have to consider YOUR business idea, the definitive idea for YOUR business, because your idea and the idea of the solution you want to use must be related in some very meaningful way!

We're coming to a very important point here:

When you're bringing a solution into your business, the solution has its own idea. That idea may be a definitive idea for the company that offers the solution (or, at least, for a part of the company), yet for you, it's just one of the ideas you're inviting into your business - under the umbrella of your own definitive idea.

It's of extreme importance to relate these two ideas - for any solution you are introducing into your company, whether you buy an external product or service, or create it internally. The right choice comes from the conceptual harmony between the two ideas that are brought together, and this is very specific for your situation and for your business.

On a side note, perhaps the biggest difficulty is that most companies don't communicate their definitive ideas precisely.

Moreover, even successful companies are often not consciously aware of their core concept. The world of ideas is not easy to navigate, and even more difficult to correlate to the world of action.

To complete the saga about the three companies, let's mention Oracle - the company that competes with them all. Even though Oracle as a company has a totally different definitive idea, they naturally moved into the application market, building the applications based on their own database layer. Their business applications division is a business within a business, and has its own definitive idea, which gracefully interplays with their original idea which created RDBMS revolution.

Logan Green (Lyft)

You would expect that Lyft and Uber were twins.

Not at all! They are far from each other, as the east from the west!

Uber is a better taxi. Much better taxi. If you use Uber once, you would hardly use a regular taxi ever again.

Does it sound like Lyft to you?

Well, let's hear out Logan Green. His definitive idea is totally different. He is eyeing elimination of car ownership. In his mind, and in the world that will eventually follow his mind, car ownership becomes irrelevant.

If you use both Uber and Lyft, you may not perceive the difference consciously. Yet, the difference is powerful and manifests on many levels and in various aspects of these great companies.

Travis Kalanick and Garrett Camp save us from the misery of using an old-fashioned taxi service. While Logan Green and John Zimmer are saving us from misery of owning a car.

This means that they don't compete. Well, they think they do, but they don't. The two companies can both be very successful. Moreover, if everything goes as conceived and planned, Lyft will become much bigger than Uber. In its extreme, the difference may be as the difference between billions of dollars and trillions of dollars. Yet, this does NOT mean that Uber will be a loser - not at all. Uber will prosper in its own right, making our lives better in its own way.

Jack Dorsey (Square)

There could be nothing simpler than this, you may think. The idea is "Accepting credit cards", right?

Well, true, this was the original idea of the founders. This is what they thought, and this is what they did.

However, with this idea, their ambitious startup couldn't close even one sale!

Fortunately for humankind, they didn't give up. They observed carefully and came to the realization that their idea was something else. As per Jack Dorsey, it's plugging a shopkeeper into the economy and enabling them to make sales - more sales, more effortless sales.

The paradox is, it's really difficult to understand how in the world such a swap of ideas can do anything for the company. After all, isn't the bottom line in them just enabling us to take credit cards?

The truth is, the power of ideas can't be understood theoretically. You have to go through it. You have to tangibly feel the energy of the ideas and how great ideas generate power.

According to Jack Dorsey, once they perceived the new idea, the world suddenly became so much bigger, so many more opportunities suddenly showed up, invisible just moments before. They started making sales. The idea affected marketing, sales, operations, offerings, everything.

Later on, when Square capital was born, a business in a business, the idea was simple again: lending, loans. What else in the world could it be?

Yet, this idea couldn't possibly work. For many reasons. Careful observation brought another idea into the world: "borrowing from a friend or a relative".

This idea changed everything. The difference was astounding. A subtle distinction between borrowing from a bank and borrowing from a friend created a new market.

Steve Jobs (Apple)

Steve Jobs revolutionized the world many times over. Yet, there was one idea, one specific concept that he developed early in life, that powerfully directed him, enabling him to see and achieve what nobody else was able to see and achieve. Again, and again. This very concept manifested itself in every stormy revolution he brought about.

He eloquently expressed this idea himself, more than once. But it wasn't so easy to extract it from everything else he said, as he said many things!

What was the concept?

A computer has immense power which can be unleashed to solve your problems. But there is one big problem between and your computer - you have to learn how to use it. Once you overcome it, the sky is your limit. This barrier must be gradually diminished, and eventually removed altogether. Removing this barrier is the priority.

Technology is able to incorporate more and more power into a computer, yet the major barrier between you and that power remains in place. We want to take that extra power and apply it toward making your interaction with a computer go smoother and easier. Eventually, the barrier will be completely removed.

Steve Jobs presented this concept on the dawn of the computer era, and remained laser-focused on it until his last day. It's really simple: taking the extra, constantly added power and use it to break the barrier. This will enable you to access the rest of the computer power intuitively and effortlessly.

"Ah, it's just user interface, why is it a big deal? Everybody was busy with user interface after all!"

No, it's not about user interface. The difference between ideas is subtle and profound. While others were busy with user interface, Steve Jobs was precisely about taking the added power and using it to break the barrier. The more the power grew, the more of that power we could take and use exclusively to break that very barrier. Steve Jobs was very limited by the power a computer had. He was very perceptive to this, and anticipated the increase in that power, which allowed him to break the barrier more and more, and even to have the solution ready by the time the additional power "arrived".

Decades ago this concept was hardly appreciated or understood. It took many difficult years and a few revolutions. The new generation now takes it for granted that an infant is literally using an iPhone or an iPad to communicate with the parents, play games, or browse media archives way before learning how to speak, without any learning curve whatsoever.

The core difference between Steve Jobs and everybody else was in internalizing this concept, making it a priority, being loyal to it, and being intensely focused on it all the time. It was this difference that powered Apple II, Macintosh II, iMac, PowerBook, iBook, MacBook, iPod, iTunes, iPhone, and iPad.

Sergei Brin, Larry Page (Google)

Sergei Brin was obsessed with the idea of making all the world's information accessible and useful. Larry Page was obsessed with downloading all the web. Both ideas were in the world of fantasy. They were unreal and unreachable at the time. Sundar Pichai summarized it later as organizing the world's information.

These are not slogans. These are actual ideas that made all the difference.

You may wonder, weren't Jerry Yang and David Filo obsessed with the same very ideas when they created Yahoo?

The answer is, no! Their idea was the idea of the guide, and all they created was the guide. They wanted to guide you through the web. No guide can masterfully guide you through the WHOLE world! The difference is subtle indeed, yet it's immense.

Open Text crawled the web, just like Google does, but on the conceptual level "the-whole-web" ambition was missing. Interestingly, this manifested in the official change of focus - they successfully evolved into enterprise search solutions. However, this change was rather an acknowledgement of what they really were to begin with, without being fully aware of it!

Being busy with lower-level ideas like guiding, curating, listing or categorizing, couldn't possibly match Google's idea. And when your idea is different, your motivation and vision are different, and your solutions are different.

Mark Zuckerberg (Facebook)

Mark Zuckerberg looked at the web, and asked a simple question: "Where are people here?"

He was the first one to ask this question. He was also the first one to take this question seriously.

Ordinary people expressing themselves on the web and connecting with each other via the web is all there is to Facebook. Once you become obsessed with such an idea, and you are intelligent and have good technical skills, you have no choice but to come up with Facebook.

The progression of ideas was logical: from representing people, to connecting people, to connecting friends, families, and groups, to bringing the world closer together, to giving people the power to build community to bring the world closer together. Building a community is a new idea, and it's a great one indeed.

If Mark Zuckerberg became obsessed with the idea of organizing the world's information, he would probably come up with Google. If Sergey Brin and Larry Page became obsessed with the idea of connecting people, they would probably come up with Facebook. But, of course, the ideas are not random. The root of the ideas people become obsessed with comes from inside, from their background and personality, from their worldview and their intellectual and emotional thirst.

Interestingly, Google's attempt to compete with Facebook failed. Why?

On the surface, Google+ was just too confusing for users. With Facebook's simplicity, it didn't have a chance.

However, this has to be understood deeper, because all Google products - with possibly one exception, Google+ - are insanely simple and intuitive to use. Simplicity is Google's credo! So, what happened to Google+? And why?

What happened was quite simple though. Google didn't bother to come up with any new ideas. Google decided to make a better Facebook. In fact, this was their definitive idea, whether they were aware or unaware.

If they had simply copied Facebook, they would, in fact, have succeeded. They would indeed have created something better than Facebook. Because they are Google!

To their bad fortune, they saw Google+ as a "better Facebook", and that "better", in their own minds, forced them to overcomplicate things and create something quite convoluted that couldn't possibly successfully compete with the simplicity of Facebook.

Here is the lesson: a sure recipe for failure is to copy somebody's idea, and then try to make a better implementation. It may only work if the one you are copying is doing something wrong, something really deficient. But if they are doing it right, you are doomed to fail, even if you are Google!

Jeff Bezos (Amazon)

Yes, Amazon is about great selection, low prices, fast and reliable delivery, but... The one idea Jeff Bezos was really obsessed with, was the idea of a happy customer. Everything else was details and implementation.

This is not to be taken lightly. This is not a marketing slogan. This is what Amazon really is – "happy customer generator"!

What about Barnes & Noble?

Their idea was, and is: "selling books". As simple as that. They tried, but failed to formulate any other great idea, hence they remained who they were - booksellers. This doesn't diminish Barnes & Noble at all; it's a great company and book-lovers love Barnes & Noble for a good reason - they love to touch books, and they love to buy books. It's such a poor and limited world when you view it in terms of winners and losers. Just because one company's market share is more, that by itself doesn't make the other company a loser!

What about Walmart?

Sam Walton said, "The secret of successful retailing is to give your customers what they want".

Is this the Walmart's idea?

Well, yes and no. Yes - because Sam Walton meant it. And no - because their understanding of what a customer wants is limited to a low price. Everything else is secondary.

And if you disagree, just shop on Amazon, and then shop in Walmart - online or offline. You'll tangibly feel the difference between the ideas.

On a side note, Jeff Bezos took advantage of the Internet at the right time. But if he didn't, if he went into brick & mortar, or anything else for that matter, with the same obsession about a happy customer, he would also, without a shadow of a doubt, experience astounding success. He would also change the world, but we now can't figure out how exactly the world would be different. Fortunately for us, he did it on the Internet, and created Amazon, the amazing phenomenon that changed our lives so much.

John Legere (T-Mobile)

With John Legere, you don't have to go too far in search of the idea. It's simple: Uncarrier! No authority matters. Rebellion. Bravery. Fearless. Fixing stupid, broken industry. Fierce opposition to Dumb and Dumber. It's all included in the brilliant term - uncarrier, which says it all.

I don't know if T-Mobile is better these days than it used to be. From my personal experience, at least in pre-John-Legere era, it was pretty bad.

But on the marketing landscape, with John Legere, the new concept behind T-Mobile transformed the company indeed.

Let me bring another example of an idea from John Legere.

First of all, I want to state clearly that I disapprove and disrespect this idea. And I am partly bringing this example to make this statement. Yes, it's brilliant indeed, though morally corrupt and intellectually dishonest.

T-Mobile came up with the plan that includes Mexico and Canada. John Legere called it Anti-Trump campaign, implying crossing the borders.

Besides being morally corrupt and intellectually dishonest, this idea demonstrates a very important principle. Definitive ideas define the companies, but at the same time, different units, parts, branches, divisions, products, various aspects or even campaigns should ideally have their own explicit ideas, under the umbrella of the main idea. And all the ideas should be interconnected in some meaningful way.

In this example, extending the area of service to Mexico and Canada is surely profitable to T-Mobile. This is not charity. Yet, extending the service is a poor concept. Not catchy. A much better concept is crossing the borders. Yet better is disregarding the borders. Even "better" is using the concept of crossing and disregarding the borders to insult the president.

I would suggest the next step for John Legere – declaring the United Unstates of America. This will take T-Mobile even higher, harmonize with Uncarrier, and surely bring plenty media attention, ultimately benefiting shareholders. After all, what else matters?

Generally, the higher a level of abstraction of an idea, and the simpler an idea is, the better.

Edward W. Stack (Dick's Sporting Goods)

In this case, the idea becomes crystal clear from the very story that led to the creation of the business.

Dick Stack was working in a local store. He loved fishing, and the owner requested Dick to bring a full list of fishing supplies. Dick enthusiastically composed the list, but the store owner rejected it, adding a negative comment. Dick grabbed the piece of paper with his list, and walked out.

No, he didn't create the business when he walked out. His grandmother did. By telling him, "Dick, always follow your dreams", she effectively created a future Fortune 500 corporation. After the encouraging words and a generous $300 "donation", he opened a storefront.

He carried fishing supplies, but if we dig for the definitive idea, we have to go a bit deeper. The idea is rooted in the conflict between Dick and his former employer. Dick knew what fishermen needed, the employer did not. His intuition failed him. The intuition of an outsider won't make him into a professional, yet, the employer was sure that he knew better than Dick.

This is it: professional counter-intuitive, skill-based, and experienced-based knowledge of what's needed, what can help, what's good - in this particular case in the fishing niche.

Later on, the company extended to other niches, and eventually became "sporting goods" retailer. Unfortunately, this generic term does a disservice, because it no longer encapsulates the essence. "Sporting" is just too wide. Besides, focusing on the concept of "sports" makes Dick's main suppliers into competitors.

The essence, and the definitive idea has never changed since the time Dick Stack quit his job. But it extended to other niches - baseball, biking, hiking, golfing, kayaking, hunting, camping, running, and so on. Pay attention - it's not just sports. It's more about active lifestyle, with the focus on one particular activity, be it sports or something else. But, what's more important it it's counter-intuitive, skill-based, experience-based knowledge - focusing on ONE NICHE AT A TIME. By taking it too wide - sporting goods retailer - they lose their advantage.

This is exactly the reason why the company is nervous about Nike, Under Armour, and Adidas selling directly to consumers. Competitors!

Well, the company itself made its major suppliers into competitors by focusing on the wrong concept. The company is misaligned with its definitive idea, presumably without being consciously aware of it.

Well, that's Dick's. But surely Nike, Under Armour, and Adidas compete, don't they?

Yes, they do. But they don't have to. Companies like to jump into the same very idea, without extending a real effort to define themselves, and then they fiercely compete with each other, fighting for market share.

The definitive concept that we are talking about is always unique. It's a unique concept that uniquely defines and identifies. Even if we go as wide as sports overall, consider the following concepts that may lead to different business activities, unique marketing messages, and distinct customer base:

- Sports is important.

- Sports is everything.

- Passion for sports.

- Better performance.

If there were four "sports" companies, with each company picking one of the four concepts and aligning itself with it, all four companies would most probably thrive, even though inevitably one of them would have the biggest market share, while the other one would have the smallest market share.

Mission or vision?

A definitive concept that we are talking about is NOT a vision, and is NOT a mission. It's just a concept. The central concept. On a level of a company, it defines the company. On a level of a company's unit, a branch, a product, an initiative, a campaign, or anything else for that matter, it defines whatever that is, and interplays with the main company's concept.

A vision is about the future, about the end result, destination.

A mission is about the impact on the society.

Of course, both, vision and mission, do correlate to the definitive concept; they have to, yet they are not it.

A company can be successful with or without explicitly perceived and formulated ideas, yet, without a shadow of a doubt, an explicitly perceived and formulated idea can take a company to the next level. Better alignment with a good idea inevitably increases the revenue and minimizes the expenses, hence making the company more profitable.

Sometimes the idea needs to be found.
Sometimes extracted.
Sometimes created.
Sometimes corrected.
Sometimes refined.
Sometimes perfected.
But never copied.

Are you ready to define yourself, to find your definitive idea, and to align all the activities with the idea, taking your life, and your business to the next level?

I'm inviting you to a conversation about your business, your industry, your competitive strategy and advantage, your unique idea, your value chain, your customers' value structure, your risks and uncertainties, your milestones, your opportunities, your problems and objectives and the best strategies that will solve your problems and meet your objectives.

https://vladtseytkin.com/contact